MW00775258

SOUL
FARM

The Purpose of
UFOs & Humans

by Steve Kim with
the Supreme Beings

COSMIC ADVICE
Alien Voice Hijacks Live TV Broadcast

I saw the subject 2012 YouTube video on December 15, 2017 for the first time, featuring a machine-generated voice of an alien, i.e., a supreme being, talking to humans in English by hijacking a live news broadcast on the Southern Television in Britain on November 26, 1977. For the age of Aquarius, the alien asked us to remove all our weapons of evil and learn to listen to a voice of inner divine self. It was no hoax. It predicted that 2014, i.e., 11+26+1977, could be a year of disclosure. It turned out to be so precise. The message itself appeared to be very stunning to humans with stake in universe. Its exact transcript follows:

"This is the voice of Vrillon, a representative of the Ashtar Galactic Command, speaking to you. For many years, you have seen us as lights in the skies. We speak to you in peace and wisdom, as we have done to your brothers and sisters all over this, your planet Earth. We come to warn you of the destiny of your race and your world so that you may communicate to your fellow beings the course you must take to avoid the disaster which threatens your world and the beings on our worlds around you. This is in order that you may share in the great awakening as the planet passes into the new age of Aquarius. The new age can be a time of great peace and evolution for your race, but only if your rulers are made aware of the evil forces that can overshadow their judgments. Be still now and listen, for your chance may not come again. All your weapons of evil must be removed. The time for conflict is now past, and the race of which you are a part may proceed to the higher stages of its evolution if you show yourselves worthy to do this. You have but a short time to learn to live together in peace and goodwill. Small groups all over the planet are learning this and exist to pass on the light of the dawning new age to you all. You are free to accept or reject their teachings, but only those who learn to live in peace will pass to the higher realms of spiritual evolution. Hear now the voice of Vrillon, a representative of the Ashtar Galactic Command, speaking to you. Be aware also that there are many false prophets and guides operating in your world. They will suck your energy from you - the energy you call money - and will put it to evil ends and give you worthless dross in return. Your inner divine self will protect you from this. You must learn to be sensitive to the voice within that can tell you what is truth and what is confusion, chaos or untruth. Learn to listen to the voice of truth which is within you, and you will lead yourselves onto the path of evolution. This is our message to our dear friends. We have watched you growing for many years as you, too, have watched our lights in your skies. You know now that we are here and that there are more beings on and around your Earth than your scientists admit. We are deeply concerned about you and your path towards the light and will do all we can to help you. Have no fear, seek only to know yourselves, and live in harmony with the ways of your planet Earth. We of the Ashtar Galactic Command thank you for your attention. We are now leaving the plane of your existence. May you be blessed by the supreme love and truth of the cosmos."

(FYI, this page is the very last page that was filled in.)

S O U L
F A R M

The Purpose of UFOs & Humans

Extraterrestrial Book for
Instant Enlightenment

**by Steve Kim with
the Supreme Beings**

SoE
Silicon Valley

SOUL FARM
The Purpose of UFOs & Humans

Book Content Written and Edited by Steve Kim with the Supreme Beings
First Page Created and Embraced by Steve Kim with the Supreme Beings
Extraterrestrial Book Published by SoE of Silicon Valley in the U.S.A.

soulfarmcontact@gmail.com

ISBN: 978-1-963308-01-3 (eBook)
ISBN: 978-1-963308-02-0 (Hardcover)
ISBN: 978-1-963308-03-7 (Paperback)

Library of Congress Control Number: 2024931626

This is a work of nonfiction.

DEDICATION

To my family, friends & soul mate,
all the guardian angels who helped me,
my late aunt who took me under her wing,
the supreme beings who have encouraged me,
and all the past/present/future souls on the earth.

CONTENTS

Dawnvolution

Revolutionized from the whole big picture of universal life system operation powered by earth-shattering core concepts, human consciousness dawned shall open up our new world.

Instant Enlightenment

This book conveys you
messages from our creators.
If you get the whole big picture,
you get enlightened as a soul farmer
and become a better person immediately.

Irony

Except for
this awesome book
and numerous textbooks,
I have hardly read a single book
from cover to cover in my life so far
although I have done a lot to stay informed.
I must have been determined to keep my brain
clear of dubious subjective information from others.
Yet, I have souled on this book project for other people.
Even so, I feel content, for this book is steadfastly objective.

Vacuity Paradox

Have we come from nothing? Shall we go back to nothing?
No, no. An egg and a sperm are not nothing, but something.
Our ashes, bones or remains are not nothing, but something.
Most of all, our eternal soul is never nothing, but something.

Acknowledgments

As a result of connecting in hindsight all those dots that I passed through in life so as to get here at this juncture of dawnvolution, I present you with an extraterrestrial book of enlightenment materials to help out our lost human souls. I hope that this fascinating book would circulate worldwide so that all the core concepts from the supreme beings could elevate our life experience in general on the earth soul farm.

After all these years, I can acknowledge the fact that all those positive or negative dots in my life were drawn by so many precious human beings who have guided me into a precise direction on long and winding roads to this juncture. Absolutely, they all turned out to be guardian angels for me. Without them, I could never even exist right here right now. As such, I am so grateful to all the souls that I encountered.

Above all, I really have to acknowledge the fact that all the supreme beings in charge of me as well as this book project have guided me closely in adopting particular words, phrases, sentences, paragraphs, chapters, and even a title of this unique extraterrestrial book while making me examine the whole big picture on the universal life system operation at almost every step of the way for a successful completion.

Without a factual direct involvement or supervision from the select group of highly determined supreme beings in charge of me and this unique extraterrestrial book project through countless exchanges of telepathic communications, I alone couldn't have written and edited this awesome book since I'm neither a trained reporter nor a professional writer. Further, I am not into philosophy, religion, science or UFO.

Yet, oddly enough, this extremely strange and weird book clearly deals with the above subjects from start to end for a lasting benefit of the entire human beings on the earth. Besides, a jump in the logic hardly exists. It is fully packed to a point that all text lines of manuscript have no room for an extra character 'o'. All critical content did not originate from me here on the earth but from them out in the universe.

Soon after composing all of 24 chapters in sequence in about nine months, I played with SkyView on my iPhone for the first time ever to discover by chance at home and at work that the supreme beings in charge of me and this book project must be on planets in the direction of the North Star aka Polaris, from where they could observe me clearly 24/7. In fact, they could view my laptop screen over my shoulder.

No wonder they have seriously taught me on a light penetration angle, for instance, utilizing assorted telepathic communication aids such as horizontal Venetian blinds, etc. It feels quite amazing as well as exciting that I even happen to know almost exactly where they are physically located in the universe. Accordingly, my acknowledgment expressed to them for their contributions holds a tangible appreciation.

Introduction

The sun is up. We all get up. The sun is down. We all get down. Why? It is because we live a life on the earth. Getting up and down is a life, or our life has ups and downs. Without exception, our life proves to be fairly complicated. For an earthly life, there are no firm road maps. As a result, we get confused and lost easily. In addition, we know little about ourselves. We don't even know who we actually are.

The situation is similar to a total blackout. Virtually no one can move freely in pitch darkness without bumping into familiar furniture or even walls in his or her own home. This is why we need a light to see where we spend our time. Stay calm and observe. The earth theater is always chaotic. We try to live a life, but we don't even know precisely why. As such, we all contribute to a chaos by doing stupid things.

It does not help. What is in the root of our problem? It is all because we were never able to do our job of solving the most puzzling questions for the human beings correctly. Who created us and why? How did we arrive here? Where are we going and when? What is the factual purpose of our existence here? For real, without knowing a correct answer to the respective questions, we're bound to be unproductive.

Actually, this bizarre, strange, weird, but fascinating project had been covert even to me for 30 years since 1984. I have devoted almost 9 years ever since November 6, 2014, to write up and edit the manuscript with the supreme beings, echoing countless extraterrestrial materials sent over to me by amazing, creative, diverse, and shocking extraterrestrial events as well as instant precise telepathic communications.

In a nutshell, this book contains all of the respective correct answers to the above most puzzling questions of the human beings. Thus, by absorbing the whole big picture on how the universal life system operates in accordance with a set of brand-new or earth-shattering core concepts exposed, any logical human beings would get enlightened right away. Armed with this knowledge, we can solve a lot of mysteries.

First, the Malaysia Airlines flight MH370 vanished on March 8, 2014. Australia, China, and Malaysia stopped search on January 17, 2017. Australia and Malaysia issued separate final reports on October 3, 2017, and July 30, 2018, admitting a failure to find the wreckage. On May 29, 2018, a 90-day private hunt was ended, too. In spite of wing parts like a flaperon found on July 29, 2015, it remains a mystery.

In this book, the entire mystery is analyzed logically. Who, why, how and whereabouts of the MH370 flight itself in the universe are dissected in an incredible extraterrestrial angle to be expounded in meticulous details outside the box. It generates a perfect sense. To leave no stone unturned, no soul of ours or theirs is perfect. Even if it were to be found later, the analysis in this book should have served a purpose.

For the sake of further clarifying the flaperon matter, two peculiar aspects seem to go against our common sense. (i) If we assume that it is indeed a piece of the Boeing 777 missing as officially confirmed by the French investigative authority on September 3, 2015, in spite of lingering doubts, how could it end up at the beach on Reunion Island when it was expected to have crashed in the southern Indian Ocean?

German oceanographers have collected information on actual Indian Ocean currents from data bottles recovered since 1864. Per their drift analysis, the flaperon must have originated from area about 2,000 miles north of the official search area off the west coast of Australia. If so, something drastic could have happened in the air above the western tip of Java Island. The flaperon could have fallen off abruptly.

(ii) It was very weird that only an entire razor-sharp trailing edge portion of the flaperon discovered at the beach was quite badly damaged with jagged remainder as if it was partially ripped or rubbed against tougher materials in force. What could have happened to the wing part portion actually? Given all the above, I could only conclude that the flaperon could have broken off against a harness over a zigzag flight.

I am pretty sure that most of you should be puzzled over what I have discussed briefly in the above with regard to the flight MH370 mystery. However, as you continue in this book, you would realize that the above mysterious case was only analyzed to illustrate or reinforce brand-new core concepts conveyed or presented to promote a well-being of the greatest number of human beings on the earth soul farm.

Incidentally in the wee hours of December 19, 2015, the supreme beings made me listen to a set of spoken words by two intermittent telepathic action orders, confirming that the MH370 flight was captured and transported by the UFO. It will not be found, but people on board are alive and well. On March 14, 2016, the supreme beings revealed to me that all three wing parts found until then were planted by people.

Second, I would talk about another baffling mystery. It's called a spontaneous human combustion which tends to crop up around the earth for real only every once in a while. The phenomenon exhibits a quick combustion of any living human body without an apparent external source of ignition. Mostly, elderly females are burned only in minutes to ashes except for their lower legs and furniture. How is it possible?

Relying on the extraterrestrial materials in this book, it could be explained dramatically, logically and thoroughly. It goes like this. A female soul takes longer to go through a set number of reincarnations until full maturity than a male soul since a woman lives longer than a man in a typical life. Thus, a male soul gets inserted into a unisex supreme body and waits long for his soul mate to become a supreme being.

However, the more he waits, the more his imperfect patience runs thin. Specifically when his one and only soul mate in the universe is fully mature, but still toils along her last phase of current reincarnated life on the earth, a subject supreme being may take a drastic measure by forcefully but painlessly ending her life with a tremendous jolt of wireless electrical energy so as to lead an eternal life together sooner.

Third, for some reason in early part of October 2016, I stumbled upon a YouTube clip on Special Head levitation. It quickly led me to Tanya & Dorise for unique street music. Within days in a seemingly-random chain of YouTube clips, I was exposed to Dynamo through Magician Impossible for the first time. His mysterious magic acts appeared entirely different from ordinary illusionary arts with learnable tricks.

It was obvious that Dynamo himself could not even explain exactly how his humanly-impossible magic worked except for hinting that he might be helped by invisible force. He appeared to have become suddenly capable of such acts while praying for three weeks in a remote forest in England. He exhibited sorcery acts with techniques such as levitation, phase, telekinesis, telepathy, teleportation, and many others.

For instance, he walked on water like a Jesus Christ, he phased himself or objects through diverse solid materials, he remotely moved objects of choice into precise directions, he surely deciphered other people's mind through their eyes, he swiftly teleported himself or objects to another place, etc. However, only the supreme beings could exercise freely the above techniques. For Dynamo's case, they did all that, too.

Seriously, the first thing the supreme beings did for Dynamo was to release a pause button on telepathic receipt portion of his spirit semi-permanently. Thus, he has been in contact with them constantly for his show to give happiness. For this arrangement, people mistake him for god or demon. Sorcery turns magic if liked, religions if believed as miracle, cult if worshiped with ulterior motive, and fraud if disliked.

Fourth, on January 26, 2017, I spotted a never-seen-before blue MOCREO power bank while vacuuming home. It wasn't ours. I asked around to no avail. It was a mystery. On February 8, 2017, I asked them and they responded with a symbolic telepathic dream. Featuring Mark Zuckerberg's invisible teleportation restroom, it verified that the supreme beings teleported it as tangible evidence of their capabilities.

Fifth, SpaceX founded by Elon Musk suffered from another loss of a Falcon 9 rocket due to a sudden explosion during preparation of a test at a Cape Canaveral launch pad on September 1, 2016. It looked so odd at the time since its engine was not even ignited. Its investigation focused on a helium system. It later claimed to have replicated a failure. Though, a real cause of the explosion seems like a mystery.

As far as I could see, these are some of the relevant facts surrounding the incident. A set of mysterious banging noise was clearly recorded way ahead of the first explosion. A sphere-shaped unidentified flying object passing directly over the rocket at a fast-supersonic speed was also recorded. A top portion of the rocket was conspicuously bulky due to a communication satellite with a laser space weapon added.

For real, the supreme beings used a drone-like UFO to destroy the rocket and its payload to prevent a space war. They banged metal parts for a spark remotely by telekinesis, but ended up firing a laser from the UFO for the detonation. Immature humans may use laser arms to shatter objects into floating debris, making a soul farm inaccessible from space. Thus they directly acted on it swiftly for a universal benefit.

Sixth, but not the last, I caught an interesting article in the Wall Street Journal dated August 26, 2015, regarding a physics professor Stephen Hawking's suggestion to solve a vexing black hole mystery. According to his fresh theory on how any radiation information could escape a black hole which even pulls in light yet releases radiation of a particle, it is not sucked in but stored in a boundary until coming out.

He asserted that a black hole boundary known as an event horizon is such place, solving an information paradox. After living a brilliant scientific life for black hole research, he plunged into one on March 14, 2018. Information on his death event was not sucked in, but stored on a time horizon. Physics respects a theory that light is fastest in the universe. Then, light is faster than time, and time is slower than light?

Science suggests that time can even be manipulated to a certain level, thus toying with a fictional time machine. However, according to the whole big picture exposed in the extraterrestrial materials given to me by the supreme beings, nothing can go faster than the speed of time in the universe. Light travels always in time, not vice versa. Simple, isn't it? It negates one of the most significant theories in our science.

When you would like to walk over to a certain place, you could be very far away from your intended destination if you start in a wrong direction to keep on walking straight. That appears to be a current status of physics on the theory. Here is a conundrum that I faced one day under a starry sky. I have communicated with the supreme beings located a set of light-years away on a real-time basis. How is it possible?

The special theory of relativity published in 1905 by the greatest theoretical physicist Albert Einstein relies on a speed of light that is absolute and constant at 186,000 miles per second and suggests that a speed of time can be relative and flexible. If so, a visual contact operation on a stream of light required for any telepathic message from the supreme beings to me should have normally taken hundreds of years.

However, it had not. It was definitely instantaneous based on a myriad of personal and real telepathic messages. For your information, the supreme beings are in the general direction toward Polaris that is at least 323 light-years away. In fact, my actual experience directly contradicts his theory. If a measurement unit of time length varies, a time period is measured flexible, but its absolute length remains the same.

Undoubtedly, the subject enlightenment information conveyed over to me by the supreme beings on July 7, 2006, unveils that the speed of time is absolute and constant while the speed of light is relative, flexible, unlimited, and instant. If so, the fastest phenomenon in the universe is not light but time. Nothing can travel faster than time to even reverse it. As such, this book is bizarre, strange, weird, but fascinating.

Yet, this book actually contains far more brand-new core concepts than necessary for helping us to merely solve some of the baffling mysteries for the earthly human beings. It successfully conveys the whole big picture with regard to the universal life system operations so that we could finally ponder over its factual content, recognize who we truly are, and change our behaviors reflecting upon what we are to do.

On October 17, 2017, I stumbled upon a small piece of information on the Internet, which was totally new to me. A seemingly-random chain of freak intellectual curiosity on English words in Dictionary.com, i.e., just, holy, and divine, led me to a term of Supreme Being used in referring to God by philosophers and theologians for Buddhism, Christianity, Hinduism, Islam, Judaism, Sikhism or some other religions.

Unlike the Supreme Being taken up dogmatically in place of a respective divinity, the supreme beings called by me precisely as such since April 5, 2014, and introduced in quite a lucid detail in this fascinating extraterrestrial project book have virtually nothing to do with any human religions. As explained logically in this book, the supreme beings are not gods but tacs. They are all imperfect beings just like us.

In fact, I called the supreme beings hastily as aliens or even robots in my enlightenment notes recorded by hand on July 7, 2006. Offhand, I just never knew a better way to call them yet. Besides, virtually every piece of information given to me was too bizarre to digest since I had absolutely no prior knowledge on the whole big picture, universal life system operations, and numerous brand-new core concepts.

Meantime, anyone could haphazardly conclude that both beings in the above contrast must be the same after all. Most religions could have mistaken the supreme beings for their gods. Regardless, they are not the same. Unlike their Supreme Being, they carry a tangible body and soul like us. Per the supreme beings, we could even become one of them sooner or later if we do the best in cultivating our own soul.

For a universal benefit of earthly affairs in harmony, I would convey you a bizarre revelation on this very project. This seemingly-weird information could trigger an eventual global movement to unify many religions into one in a way. As I stated clearly at the end of the last chapter in this book, I myself have absolutely no interest or stake in any religion. This quite a story takes us to the North Star like a fairy tale.

As expressed, I innately became fully aware of their actual planetary existence in the general direction of Polaris by working with them directly for real on this book project. Even so, they had never disclosed the following story to me until June 21, 2016. I fell asleep at desk with my laptop on. They shook my shoulder madly at 4:00 a.m. for a lecture on the North Star in a random YouTube clip then being played.

A comparative religion philosopher Hong-Sik Yoon revealed the story. Per celestial information brought by his mentor Bong Woo from an association located near Polaris, the third and last 60-year prep phase for a global revolution in human consciousness was started in 1984 to end in 2044. A 1954-born Korean of 1/3 from the north and 2/3 from the south would do the job with a key frame to be had by 2014.

A verbatim lucidity for key factors to open up a new world shocked me. They talked about me? I shivered a bit. I was born in 1954 with Korean blood of 1/3 from the north and 2/3 from the south. I came to America right after 1974. I saw my first UFO in 1984. I received such frame in 2014. They made me a human consciousness coordinator in 2017. Our past seems by design. I am so curious about our future.

ONE:

Upshot of Truth vs. Fact

If you build a house, a solid foundation must be first. All human beings ought to be a unique animal. In daily life, they believe nothing unless it is known to be true or factual. How so? It is because their belief system by design accepts only truth and/or fact. What are they in terms of definitions? How are they different? Concluding from a cursory review, many dictionaries offer little definitive help if not confusion. People mostly remain disengaged. Without clarifying those two confusing words first, you can't even begin to grasp the purpose of UFOs and humans. Let's do something about it.

Drop everything and stare at the sky. Did you do it? Go do it now and come back. Well, assuming you actually viewed the sky with your own eyes just now, I will ask you related questions. In order to observe the sky, did you raise your head or lower it down? What did you do? What kind of posture did you take to scan the sky? Did you look up or look down? Please think about what you did exactly in fact.

When requested, most people tend to gaze at the sky above their head. Very few people would look for it below their head. Even though they are already situated way up in the air such as on a hot air balloon, on top of a mountain, in a passenger airliner or in a skyscraper, they would still raise their head at least a bit to stare at a higher place way above. Why? Why not look for the sky in the lower places as well?

Undoubtedly, the sky should be located everywhere. Before delving further from this rather uncustomary remark, let's get one thing straight reflecting on our own earthly life. Most human behavior patterns stem from inborn instinct or acquired habit. All the human beings on the earth are either programmed prior to birth to behave in a certain manner or conditioned later as such through education and experience.

Physically, the sky is part of the universe. The earth that is surrounded completely by the same sky is part of the universe, too. Then, all the seemingly-empty space visible to or even touchable by the earthlings and located above or below their head also belongs to the sky and to the universe. Accordingly, the sky is everywhere. In fact, based on logic, we live on the earth, in the sky, and actually in the universe.

Does the sky have a limit? For that matter, does the universe have a limit? If you stretch out the sky beyond the earth environment, the same sky gets totally blended in the universe. Then, the whole thing is limitless simply because nobody on the earth has discovered yet a solid boundary of the universe for once. As a result, virtually everyone would relentlessly believe as the truth the universe being limitless.

The big bang theory rules the earth. Catholic priest & astronomer Georges Lemaitre asserted a single explosion as the origin of the universe in 1927, but orbiting directions of stars or planets aren't identical to the explosion direction. How about the big box theory? Dense smoke gushes out of a big box, expanding into a bigger box that does not expand. This new theory explains direction irregularity in the above.

According to the supreme beings, truth may change, but fact does not. A precise understanding of it or lack of it affects outcome. For instance, examine a case for Nicolaus Copernicus. He bumped into the new truth that the earth is revolving around the sun, never the other way around. His astronomy and mathematics research results touted the fact, overturning the truth for the universe prevailing at the time.

For another instance, examine a case of Adolf Hitler. He carried out an extermination of six million Jews judged by German scientists as an inferior race. A twist of Charles Darwin's theory on survival of the fittest culminated in the ridiculous systematic gene pool cleanup. The Nazis fooled by the false truth of racial superiority ended up committing the Holocaust. The fact is that all humans are created equal.

Now, let's think about all the stars in the sky. Once the sun is up, night stars transform into day stars which are invisible to our eyes due to the sun much closer thus shinier. It does inject an unimaginable amount of light into the earth atmosphere. Nonetheless, all those same stars are still there occupying the same space. Despite lots of people assuming otherwise haphazardly, they don't simply disappear from it.

Regardless of visibility, the stars are in the sky night and day. By the same token, the very existence of an object has fundamentally nothing to do with a sighting by humans. If it exists, it exists. If it doesn't, it doesn't. In fact, all the physical objects including UFOs and the supreme beings do not have to be endorsed by humans after a sighting in order to exist. A human acknowledgment would not matter at all.

Meanwhile, please look up respective definitions of truth and fact in your own English dictionary to completely understand their accurate meanings and distinctive concepts. A whole mess of vaguely descriptive thus utterly confusing definitions may be found in many dictionaries. This is why their precise definitions were also included in the July 2006 enlightenment materials, which I would tell you again later.

Whenever a gap develops between a truth and a fact for any reason, the truth would have to be changed in order to resolve the gap because the fact could not be changed by its nature. Consequently, people involved would generally need to make a personal choice on what to believe, i.e., the new truth vs. the old fake truth. Escaping uncertainty, most people would love to settle quickly with the easiest way out.

Due to this advanced character of our human nature searching for a shortcut or way out utilizing the least effort, expert opinions would play a significant role in any society. Forgoing a direct personal examination, most people would simply rely on a select set of expert opinions on an incident, issue, matter or subject. However, no one is always perfect. No experts are immune from making a mistake in judgment.

When any type of a critical mistake however big or small is made, it may eventually find its way into triggering a discord among the expert opinions, and the situation may quickly develop into a sort of full-blown controversy. If so, people tangled up might have to pull themselves together to sort things out, thereby falling into an intellectual turmoil at least for a while until the real truth wins over the fake truth.

Come to think of it, all human beings could open or close their mind to external stimulus on any given occasion as they wish, thus contributing to an eventful picture of the opinionated society as a whole. Gradually and quietly over time, most human beings would willingly mold themselves into displaying a consistent character described generally as open-minded, closed-minded, somewhere in the middle, etc.

For each and every human being, a degree of certain openness in one's mind could fluctuate at any moment case by case. It means that people could change their own mind anytime depending on how each new encounter is unfolded and absorbed. Meanwhile, by definitions, any truth should be the real truth if it proves to be in full conformity with the underlying fact. Any truth not belonging to the fact dies off.

No matter what happens in our life, if possible, it is definitely more rational to get to the bottom of the fact than just to scuttle around any truth which could even be labeled as the untruth in the worst case. While any fact is objective and certain, any truth is subjective and capricious due to an inherent volatile property of human interpretations involved. Hence it is only prudent to pursue the fact beyond any truth.

Oftentimes, as illustrated, there could even be more than one truth at the same time opposing each other, yet the fact would remain intact as one forever since it does simply represent a correct picture of something that actually exists or has happened. If the truth turns out to be no longer valid, it would certainly be wise to do away with the old truth and adopt the new truth, thereby conforming directly to the fact.

At this point, I would like to tell you a bit about me. I am just an ordinary man, neither too bright nor too stupid. Although I am about to touch upon all these weird subjects regarding the universal life system, three separate sightings of unidentified flying objects, my enlightenment experience, and many other astounding extraterrestrial events or things, I have hardly sought for them. Instead, they barged into me.

Before the actual sighting of a gigantic flying saucer hovering low directly over my head in complete silence for a relatively long period in broad daylight while exposing its minute details such as small rivets fastening together many aluminum-like panels covering a huge dome-shaped bottom, I was always an absolute nonbeliever. However, ever since, I have known firsthand that UFOs do in fact exist around us.

Accordingly, it is an irony, but I have found myself not terribly interested in the whole subject regarding UFOs. I am indeed seldom curious about or surprised by any such UFO stories since I know precisely not only their existence but also their purpose of visiting the earth. Moreover, I am not a UFO expert, but I understand I am kind of required to tell you so many things I happen to know. Strange, is it not?

Except for my subliminal hunch, I still do not know for sure why the supreme beings handling the project chose me to absorb, analyze, communicate, encounter, experience, learn, observe, ponder, publish, realize, receive, send, speak, summarize, and write with regard to what I am supposed to convey you in this strange book. Perhaps, I got selected for a reason since I am neither a religious person nor a scientist.

Obviously, the supreme beings would not possess a prejudice against any religious persons and scientists per se. However, their own personal and professional stubbornness cultivated in a fairly closed environment requiring absolute illogical trust or authenticated scientific proof, respectively, and their own resultant limitations might prevent them from conveying you intact all the facts on extraterrestrial matters.

On the other hand, maybe, I got only selected for no particular reasons except that I happened to be at the wrong place at the wrong time to begin with, i.e., at the moment of my initial UFO sighting. If then, I should really be a wrong person to do this incredible job for them, for I am neither a trained reporter nor a professional writer. Regardless, they have forced me so hard into this amazing confessing corner.

So far, to me, these are the facts. They exposed the gigantic UFO to me in 1984, brought my just-passed-away aunt to me as a 3-D figure in 2004, enlightened me as to the universal life system operations through a telepathic mail in 2006, imprinted two UFOs on retina in my left eye in 2008, transported the missing Malaysian flight MH370 out of the earth in 2014, and revealed to me yet another UFO in 2014.

On my way of describing the MH370 case as above, although practically most of you might have a strong doubt, I would soundly classify it as the fact beyond a mere theory. I could, should, and would tell you what happened, not just what might have happened. Anyone having the same set of critical information and extraordinary insight that I happen to possess should reach the same logical conclusion as I did.

Of course, all out-of-the-earth factual elements that I listed chronologically in the above would be hard or even incomprehensible for anyone to bite off, chew, and swallow to believe some or all as the truth at a respective face value, let alone trusting them as the fact. I could not fathom what the consequences of this project would be, but bear with me for now until we will all be there to open up our new world.

Now, let us get on with a special journey to find out a factual purpose of UFOs visiting the earth and of humans inhabiting the earth. Armed with not only the truth but also the fact, we would finally be able to answer correctly on the most puzzling questions for the entire human beings: Who created us and why? How did we land here? Where are we going and when? What is the purpose of our existence here?

TWO:

The Earth Is a Soul Farm

Onto the solid foundation on upshot of truth vs. fact, you are ready to erect a strong frame of the house securely. Nevertheless, it might be extremely hard for most all of you to fully digest any of these brand-new thus earth-shattering core concepts revealing our human origin since they would be too hard to bite off and chew, let alone swallowing them. However, if you keep in mind that a good medicine usually tastes bitter, you would be able to endure personal anguish in trying to understand the whole big picture with virtually no holes in it. You could also simply walk away if you wish.

Have you ever wondered about human origin per se? Until I got suddenly enlightened very clearly on the subject in a bizarre way in 2006, I had wondered about it from time to time, but my answer to the puzzle had been quite simple like the one from Socrates in ancient Greece – I don't know. Paraphrasing his words, he used to advise, "Wisdom begins with wonder. I know that I know nothing. Know yourself."

During the Memorial Day weekend in 2005, I went camping with a friend of mine at Yosemite National Park in California for a demanding hike to Half Dome. To this day, I could recall vividly what I saw in the sky during one night. Away from bright camp lights sprinkled, it was pitch-black at the side of the mountain floor except for the dazzling sky. With the moon off, it was tightly packed with shining stars.

Until then, I had never been even able to visualize a well-known fact about the universe that the sky contains an unthinkable number of shining stars regardless of visibility to the earthly human beings. Located in a remote corner of the vast universe, the earth is never even a genuine star but only a tiny obscure planet remotely circling around the sun which happens to be the nearest shining star from the earth.

By the way, the sun is the only star absent from our night sky forever. The sun is apparently a star, too, but it is visible only during the daytime, being totally different from all the other stars. It is all fact. However, it is a little weird, isn't it? If you think about it on a universal scale, the earth along with the universe is full of all kinds of unknown stuff as well as all sorts of known stuff irrespective of weirdness.

Even if we collect all the information pieces known to humans scattered everywhere on the earth, store them in a central computer database while eliminating all duplicates, and add them up for a total in a definitive measurement unit, it should still be far smaller than a total for all the unknown information pieces to be discovered or explored by all of us with inherent curiosity. As such, we are still quite ignorant.

Obviously, the unstoppable worldwide proliferation of the awesome high-speed Internet in the last decade or so has certainly contributed to the accelerated development of our modern human civilizations in general. It has provided an effective, efficient, practical, and sophisticated means of masterfully disseminating a variety of intellectual materials covering the full spectrum of cumulative human experience.

Meanwhile, as mentioned above, when we compare the amount of all the known knowledge pieces available so far on the earth to that of all the unknowns, only if possible even to guesstimate, there must be virtually no comparison just like a tiny drop in a coffee mug now and probably ever because for sure we usually have absolutely no idea on how much we do not even know yet on almost any given subject.

For instance, according to a pharmaceutical industry news article issued in 2013, out of about 6,000 rare diseases known to humans so far, doctors could treat only up to 200 to 300 with pharmaceutical products. In other words, a vast majority of those sick patients suffering from such dreadful diseases might never even be properly treated. There must be a colossal pile of the unknowns in the medical field, too.

Now, let's get back to the earth where all the known human beings to us in the entire universe have inhabited for a relatively short period of time. Precisely how short is that? Frankly speaking, we do not even know that since we could only come up with a rough estimate at best due to a lack of tangible human arrival records located on the earth. Arrival? Within the context of universal life system, we arrived here.

Why so? It is solely because the earth is a soul farm. Our earth is one of their soul farms operated in the universe. Who are they? Based on what I was given at my incredible instant enlightenment, they are our original creators, period. Are they gods? Per their revelation, they are not gods at all. Gods are intangible, reside only in mind, and cannot create tangible humans. Our original creators are totally different.

I surely understand that most all of you cannot even process what I have just started to tell you step by step with complete honesty. The whole content to the end should be drastically different from what has been assumed widely on the earth. Regardless, all these new core concepts that I am required to bring you are not only the truth but also the fact according to them. I am simply running an errand for them.

Let's keep moving deeper into the whole big picture so as to solve all the puzzling questions for the human race. Hence, who are our creators? Are they related to any UFOs? Oh, any UFOs per se are not relatives of their own creators, but their space travel vehicles. It happens that our creators would frequently ride in them or occasionally control them remotely for tasks. Our earthly drones are similar in a way.

What? How is it possible? In the whole big picture, those mysterious UFO riders physically created our original body and soul to meet their need. We were kept in the dark. Accordingly, we have called them in very ambiguous terms like aliens, E.T.s, extraterrestrials, outer space beings, outer space visitors, space aliens, space beings, space inhabitants, space visitors, etc. It indicates how frustrated we have been.

Well, then, don't we already know them? Of course, many people aside from me have even sighted them for real, according to them. Some of them even claimed further that they had been actually abducted for unknown reasons to be returned later. To keep the record straight, I never actually sighted any UFO riders in person, but I picked up clues that they were clearly present at two of my three UFO sightings.

Human confusion and frustration toward them were caused by our evasive, fearful, insecure, undecided, unsure, and vague attitude not prone to acknowledge their existence, let alone appreciating their genuine efforts to visit our earth. To eliminate uncertainty, I would keep referring to them as the supreme beings as I have so far. Furthermore, it is only accurate, just, and proper since they are our creators in fact.

Now, then, who created our own creators originally? According to the supreme beings, it should never be our job, but their job to go after such a question. Our own concerns should end with solving our own puzzle for the human race. It is like a computer asking us about our origin. Practically, I do not dare to persuade all of you hearing about what I am trying to convey. It is indeed your job to take it in or pass it.

Serenely, I am contemplating the whole earth again in a beautiful NASA photo taken from the space in the past. It sure looks mostly blue with some white, brown and green due to sunlight being reflected on respective oceans, clouds, and continents. It comes across as perfectly round in shape. However, only its daytime side is visible, and it is so pretty. No wonder it is called the blue marble. Nature is awesome.

While appreciating the pretty blue marble protruded in the middle of the pitch-dark space filling the background of the photo, I am pondering about the human beings living sporadically on continents and islands. Although provision shortages could affect a future trend, since the arrival of the very first set of modern humans to the earth, our population has kept growing and growing with virtually no limitations.

Without exception, all the live human beings on the earth do possess both body and soul. I have never heard of any live human beings possessing either body or soul alone. Even an injured or sick patient clinging to life on a hospital bed in a vegetative condition possesses both body and soul. If a soul leaves a body, the soul alone is not a human being. Certainly, a human being with no soul is not alive but dead.

With no exception, all the human bodies born on the earth are created by a dramatic meeting of a female egg and a male sperm to happen in a female womb by way of sexual intercourse mostly or in a test tube with in vitro fertilization. An egg, sperm, and womb are all human body parts, period. If so, what about Jesus Christ? What about him? His body was also created and born in the same usual manner in fact.

Now, let us combine all three facts presented above. There have been always more and more people on the earth. Everybody alive on the earth possesses both body and soul. Meeting of female egg and male sperm produces only body. Then, logically, we should be puzzled and disturbed a little. What about souls? While more bodies were made up by us, where did all the additional souls required for us come from?

So weird, isn't it? Evidently, we did not make them. Even if diverse savvy engineers, programmers, researchers, scientists, technicians, and so forth would keep on working diligently forever with artificial intelligence, nobody could ever produce a single soul in either laboratories or factories on the earth, which would be totally identical with the souls that the supreme beings produced there and distributed here.

In fact, such is our reality. It is not that we discount seemingly-unlimited professional talents found on the earth, but that a task of making a brand-new soul is fundamentally beyond our capability. Let's imagine that we could turn an artificial intelligence developed utilizing the most advanced technology with deep learning, fuzzy logic, sixth sense, etc. into a soul. Could we exclusively put it into a human fetus?

With our earthly limitations, it is entirely impossible. All human beings would never be able to do so. How come? It is simply because we are not them. Then, can they pull it? Yes, of course, the supreme beings have been doing it ever since they created the human beings originally for a reason. Other pertinent critical facts should be introduced right here in order to put together the whole big picture on soul farms.

As briefly mentioned before, all gods can exist only within a soul due to their intangible thus invisible character. They cannot be present by themselves in the physical world on the earth and in the universe for that matter. As a result, we have never seen any real gods walking around among us. Instead, countless invisible gods have been created in mind and deeply revered by all kinds of people in diverse culture.

Unlike all such gods, the supreme beings have their tangible thus visible character in the form of body and soul just like us, but they exhibit different body types from ours. Per eyewitness accounts, they are hairless, naked, short and thin. Two big eyes are on head; six fingers may be on hand. I don't disagree. Oddly, we may feel a sense of sixth finger while counting fingers spread on a surface with eyes closed.

Most likely, their body is built that way to withstand routine interplanetary travels in diverse or harsh conditions without employing spacesuits and telescopes. On the other hand, according to them, they possess exactly the same soul as ours. The only difference lies in a maturity level of each soul in their body. All of their souls are fully mature while all of our souls display a wide range of maturity in progress.

Much like the human beings multiplying themselves, the supreme beings do multiply themselves in own way, too. They achieve it by manufacturing, not by childbirth, though. They manufacture bodies and souls at their factories, but all those souls cannot be used at once since they are blank with no unique content cultivated in free will to discern. So they use soul farms to mature them, and the earth is one of such.

THREE:

I Saw a Gigantic UFO (1)

Even in broad daylight in the middle of a busy place, if you happen to detect an immense unearthly round object hovering right above your head out of the blue, you may be paralyzed a bit due to complete awe. Nonetheless, after the extraordinary episode gets to be over, you would attempt to recall everything your instinct must have picked up even on a subconscious level. As for me, I still remember vividly all those minute details on the gigantic UFO witnessed in 1984. So I have been quite consistent in telling my story to others, but I have never contacted any authorities or organizations.

During your current lifetime on the earth, you get to experience by design all sorts of different things regardless of who you are, where you are, and what you do. However, you are bound to forget insignificant details as time goes by. With a limited capacity of your brain, you do not remember everything forever unless each memory is kept permanently in the long-term memory data warehouse within your brain.

Once more, I'm about to recall one of my long-term memory pieces engraved and stored in my brain for over 30 years. Hopefully, it would lead me to all the other memory pieces related to the overwhelming event one by one so that I could tell you all about my abrupt real-life encounter with a gigantic UFO. I can't forget about it so long as I live, for I clearly experienced it. As such, the whole thing is factual.

To the best of my memory, the incident in San Jose, California, happened back in 1984. Unfortunately, I cannot pinpoint an exact date of the year due to a missing calendar on which I must have drawn by habit a tiny graphic symbol for such an unusual experience. However, I still remember the entire episode in detail from start to end so vividly as if the incredible incident took place just a few hours ago or so.

Except for three years serving in the U.S. Army and two years wrapping up college at UC Berkeley, I had lived in the South Bay area of the northern California since 1975 prior to the incident. The area includes the city of San Jose surrounded by more than ten satellite cities. It is also called Silicon Valley, a world capital of high-tech industry, where several millions of people work for thousands of companies.

At the time, I was working as one of the auditors for the Defense Contract Audit Agency of the U.S. Department of Defense. Our branch office used to process all the audit workloads relating to many big or small defense contractors located in our responsibility section of Silicon Valley. As a result, I usually spent most of my time working in the field here and there. That particular day was no exception to me.

After work I was heading home directly from one of the defense contractors situated somewhere in the northern section of San Jose. For some reason, I decided to use local streets to get home instead of taking freeways as usual. As such, I was going straight on Monterey Road from north to south in general. Barely crawling inch by inch, I was stuck in a bad bumper-to-bumper traffic for a long time as I recall.

Due to a multitude of accident scenes along the way, I could only move at an average speed of six miles per hour. One of real dangers in having to drive too slowly for long is that it is so easy for anybody to fall asleep behind the wheel. In no way, I was an exception. Pretty soon, I became bored. I started to feel drowsy, too. In a hurry, I practically had to come up with a doable way to escape from such a nuisance.

Instantaneously, I grabbed my steering wheel firmly with both hands and began to gaze intensively at the sky in front of my car heading south. Soon I found myself paying attention through the windshield to quite a few bright white lights heading north at certain intervals along a straight line in the blue sky. Because the line sat directly over Monterey Road I was on, I felt all the lights were coming towards me.

If you read a road map for San Jose, California, you could see that the San Jose International Airport is situated in the middle of the northern section of the city to the south of the great San Francisco Bay. Also, you could easily see that the general direction of all the airport runways roughly coincides with an imaginary straight line extended from the north end of Monterey Road also called Monterey Highway.

Meanwhile, approximately 60 miles prior to landing at the airport, regular passenger airliners from Los Angeles to San Jose should start descending from a cruising altitude of at least 30,000 feet. Soon, they should lower all landing gears including a set of bright headlamps installed on top of the front wheels. This landing preparation maneuver would explain all of the bright white lights. They were headlights.

At any rate, my own little impromptu to free myself from dozing off at the wheel while I was stuck for long in a bad traffic jam that day worked out really fine. Actually, it was a little fun to fixate my eyes on one of those oncoming bright white lights and follow it through intently across the sky for a couple of minutes till it subsequently disappeared from my windshield. It certainly made me stay wide awake.

Soon after, I would steadily focus my eyes onto the next target in line to do the same thing all over again while driving carefully. I wasn't actually counting the number of those bright white lights which I did finish having fun with. However, it should have been around ten or so before I met this last one probably by chance. It was undeniably strange. It appeared exactly the same as others, but it wasn't moving.

For real, I was moving to it bit by bit instead of both moving closer to each other at a certain combined speed as expected. As I suddenly realized this conspicuous aspect of it compared to all the previous bright white lights, I tried to reassure myself over and over by paying a serious attention to keep track of its surroundings down below on the ground. The more I became convinced, the more I became confused.

Naturally, I started paying even more attention to it. Of course, other bright white lights were still passing in the sky as before, but I found myself ignoring them completely. Curiously enough, there was another conspicuous aspect to it. It was floating in the air without moving, but its altitude was significantly lower than the set flight path for the other lights. At one point, I thought of it as one of the streetlights.

However, it was purely a judgment error on my part since it was actually floating a lot higher in the air than any streetlights near the vicinity of it down below on the ground. There was simply no comparison at all. Besides, it was too early to turn any streetlights on. Even after I had struggled with the going-home traffic for so long, there was still a lot of sunlight left. It must have been late summer or early fall.

As I steadily advanced closer, it still remained at the same exact aerial spot way up in the sky. For certain, I was hit with all kinds of thoughts as to what it possibly could be. I knew I was good at brainstorming, but I couldn't come up with any other plausible idea than the streetlight possibility that I had ruled out early on. With my eyes fixated intently all onto it, I must have driven at least twenty more minutes.

Just like an awful lot of automobiles on the street at the time, my car didn't have a sunroof, either. Accordingly, the windshield was the only lookout through which I could observe the sky in front of my car while going forward. So, as I finally reached the vicinity below the bright white light, it eventually disappeared from my windshield, but I kept on driving, debating with myself whether to stop my car or not.

Once I realized that I was just about to pass through the spot right below the weird bright white light which had to be still floating way up, I promptly decided to stop there at once to take a look up-close in person. Immediately after passing a small intersection of Skyway Drive and Monterey Road, I quickly veered off to the right of the local road and stopped my car on a dirt area right next to the railroad track.

Union Pacific Railroad track between San Francisco and Los Angeles was laid there in parallel to the immediate west of Monterey Road. Back then, the street was not fully developed so a tiny patch of land beyond the street shoulder to the railroad track was not paved at all. Meanwhile, after losing a sight of it from my windshield, only about a couple of minutes had passed before I stopped to get out of my car.

As I still recall vividly, due to a sudden shock, I did not even have a chance to shut the driver side door properly as I was getting out of my car. As soon as I raised my neck to observe the sky right above my head, I got almost frozen. Instead of the bright white light that I was expecting to find, I was looking at a gigantic round thing. To my big surprise, it covered up more than one half of the entire sky above me.

While I could not observe it continuously due to its eventual disappearance off my windshield, the bright white light must have descended quite a vertical distance from its original altitude in a hurry so as to be floating at a very low level of the sky. Also, at the same time, it must have turned off the bright white light that I was supposed to take a look, revealing a complete body of the gigantic round something.

Why? At the time, there was no way of figuring out an answer to such a question, for it turned out to be the very first dot to be connected with many other peculiar dots later. In hindsight, it had taken me 29 years before I could finally sit down, connect all those dots for the first time, and make a current, complete, and accurate sense out of the whole set on September 1, 2013. Recently, it's made a lot more sense.

Let's ponder upon these follow-up questions. What was a real purpose for the gigantic floating object to initiate an abrupt, drastic, precise, and speedy drop in altitude right before I parked my car? How could it figure out in advance if, when, and where I should ultimately stop to get out? All these analytical questions already point in one direction for an answer. Oddly, the object wanted to expose itself to me.

Further, the object even turned off its blinding light for me to observe it so clearly. Even though a considerable number of loose eyeballs were present near the intersection in broad daylight, it took a big risk against general sighting and did what it did so swiftly. Certainly, its whole purpose should have been far more important than its calculated risk. For me, I didn't know a thing at the time. I was in the dark.

On the other hand, whatever it was up to at the time, it could have been conducting its duties, independent of me. In other words, I could have never been figured into its own sudden moves which should have been a direct result of its own risk analysis before initiating such actions. Who cares? After all, as introduced briefly before, I was just one of the ordinary human beings to reside and work in Silicon Valley.

Moreover, until then, I had absolutely nothing to do with anything mysterious such as extraterrestrials or UFOs including space or universe for that matter. In fact, I never possessed the slightest idea on any such subjects. Due to a lack of interest, I didn't even view a single episode of 'Star Trek', for example, from start to finish. My rare exceptions were 'Close Encounters of the Third Kind' and 'Star Wars'.

Come to think of it now after all these years, the one I encountered for real in broad daylight at the streets of San Jose seemed to be probably as big as the one featured in the 1977-released classic movie 'Close Encounters of the Third Kind', but it didn't look as glittering or sophisticated as the one shown in an epic scene of the Steven Spielberg's movie. Nevertheless, I was in shock during my actual sighting of it.

If a level of shock goes beyond a certain limit upon encountering a gigantic unearthly object, it quickly triggers complete awe that instantly freezes your body and soul a bit. Right away, nothing else becomes more important than the current incident. However, afterwards, you try to recall and remember all the details. As for me, I feel like I could still come up with a detailed drawing of the gigantic UFO I saw.

FOUR:

I Saw a Gigantic UFO (2)

In 1984, I did not just see a mysterious bright white light floating high up in the blue sky. It was stationary, but it quickly descended to a quite low level and proved to be a gigantic UFO. Until then, I had not believed in such UFOs. I had been wrong, dead wrong. It made me soberly humble. I ought to be nothing but a speck of dust lost in the universe. The incredible encounter turned out to be only a beginning. Ever since, I have experienced quite diverse extraterrestrial events that barged into my life. I have never asked for them. On the gigantic UFO itself, the fact is that I saw it up-close.

It was not surreal. It was real. Even so, I felt like it was surreal as if I had found myself on a Hollywood movie set. To be sure, I was not in a science fiction movie, but in a lively high-tech industrial area nicknamed Silicon Valley. Standing right next to my car with the driver side door ajar, I happened to be positioned directly below a gigantic thing. Yes, it sure was a thing. Yet, I had never seen such a thing.

I had no idea on what it was. In fact, throughout an entire duration of the encounter, I had no time to figure out what it was. Apparently, my instinct was not allocating any of my precious time to figuring out such a thing. Instead, it was letting me observe whatever it was carefully, discreetly, and rather thoroughly at least on a subconscious level since I was virtually frozen from the very outset of the encounter.

Luckily, I was already quite proficient in observing things in general because I was able to acquire and sharpen a sort of trained eye while working as a government auditor. As I recall, I used to carry out any observing duty seriously with a mindset of total emptiness found on a blank piece of paper so to speak. That way, I used to absorb like a sponge as much raw information as I could for an accurate analysis.

Believe it or not, critical information seems to have its own set of legs. If you set aside a sufficient empty space in brain, it walks in to assist you later when the time comes. Otherwise, it won't. Then, you will have to work without it, exposing yourself to committing a crucial mistake in report. So, early on in my professional career, I learned fast how to become a dolt right away while encountering anything new.

The gigantic thing floating right above my head was not an exception in that regard. As expressed so far, it was something definitely bizarre or eerie. Although my body as well as my soul was not functioning properly mainly due to complete awe, my animalistic instinct began working on its own to push me, i.e., an instant dolt with an empty space in brain, into observing anything and everything on the object.

The thing was gigantic. It was not small. It was not big. It was not huge. To me, at least, it was surely gigantic. Since I was directly below a dead center of the round thing, I bent my neck all the way to the back and twisted it around to rotate in all different directions as needed while trying to observe the whole thing in details. From my vantage point, it was covering up slightly over 50 percent of the entire sky.

The thing was stationary. It was levitating freely up in the air, but not moving or shaking at all. Of course, there was no heavy equipment like a super-sized crane nearby to pull it up so high with its long-stretched arm called a boom. Accordingly, somehow, it was clearly not being dangled up. It was unbelievable. How could it be? How was it possible? My instinct tacitly signaled me that it was simply unearthly.

Come to think of it now, I did not even feel a slight streak of any downdraft during the whole encounter, either. Even without powerful downward streams of compacted air from the round thing, it was still able to remain at the same aerial position fairly low. In my estimation, it was floating or levitating at only about 100 feet above the ground, which was even lower than the top of a standard 10-story building.

The thing looked anti-gravitational. What is gravity? Within the confines of the earth environment, it's simply an attractive force which pulls anything and everything toward a center of the earth. Theoretically, nobody or nothing can escape from it without a set of wings or mechanical devices. However, the thing seemed to defy or offset the gravity in a cinch with a technology exotic to the earthly human beings.

Certainly, the thing was continuously activating the neat antigravity feature which was beyond our engineering, scientific, and technological capabilities. I sensed it at once. It was so obvious. Evidently it was one of the main reasons why I got succumbed to complete awe and virtually frozen solid on the spot at the beginning of the awesome encounter. I was shocked to watch such a technology in action for real.

Right in front of my eyes, such a surreal technology was not only being proven as real, but also being put to use for real, specifically in our earth atmosphere as well. Wow! Even to this day, just to recollect upon what I witnessed on the fateful day brings me a unique excitement and hope for humanity. It should be a matter of figuring out a seemingly complex but actually simple scientific code outside the box.

Actually, we human beings do currently possess all sorts of flying or levitating apparatus such as airplane, hang glider, helicopter, hot air balloon, rocket, space shuttle, etc., which make use of some part of the antigravity technology. Unfortunately, none of those are fast enough, quiet enough, safe enough, and above all good enough. Even for the case of helicopter that could fly or float in the air, it is too noisy.

The thing was quiet. I could be totally wrong, but it seemed to have no moving parts inside the thing because it was maintaining a complete silence with no such repetitive mechanical noise as frictional sound breaking out of it at all. For your understanding, I did not have a hearing problem in my ears. For that matter, I wasn't experiencing any sensory deprivation phenomenon, either. It was simply so noiseless.

The thing was clean. Even though it was floating or levitating in the sky for a relatively long period of time, i.e., at least several minutes or so per my estimation in my mind at the time, it was not spewing out a single trace of exhaust fumes. Being quite familiar with nasty jet fumes spreading around near airport runways, it was very refreshing that the thing was not generating any pervasive odor while in action.

The thing was round. As far as I could judge, it was perfectly round in general shape, suggesting succinctly that it was quite methodically and meticulously manufactured in an industrial complex. In the meantime, it was not spinning or turning during its unique exposure. Interestingly, it was the same way during its uncanny departure maneuvers, too. As a result, I could observe its whole body in quite a detail.

For a while, I could only see the bottom of the thing because it was floating up in the sky and also because I had to look straight up from the ground. During an observation, I could recognize its grey skin materials to a certain degree. It appeared to be tightly covered with aluminum-like panels of different geometrical patterns. They were all fastened up with small rivets at regular intervals. I saw them so clearly.

There was a huge dome drooping upside down from the middle portion occupying most of a flat round disk area which boasted a diameter of at least 200 feet or even longer. For your information, a total wingspan of a jumbo airplane is about the same or shorter. It is tricky to compare the two properly since there is a drastic difference in mass between a sphere and a cross. It must have been a huge jumbo thing.

Around a curved round peripheral edge of a dome at the bottom of the thing, I was able to observe a fair number of conspicuous light bulbs flickering in respective colors of blue, green, red, yellow, and so forth. At the time, I noticed that actual light bulbs were solidly installed with no covers. I could not and did not count them. A quarter century later, I realized that actual colors looked tacky or unsophisticated.

The whole dome itself making up a bottom half of a sphere seemed to have no mundane parts like landing gears to be lowered down. Noticeably, it was mostly covered up with a multitude of pizza-shaped panels curved. Of course, the thing could not have been a drone for certain, for such a machine was hardly even thought of on the earth at the time. All the man-made drones are a lot smaller and fairly recent.

Out of the blue, the thing began to move. Finally, it was moving away from the scene. The departure mode was abrupt, decisive, shocking, spectacular and above all unique. To my complete surprise, the whole thing swung to the left on an arc within one second to be frozen at a resultant angle only for a split second before making its consecutive swing to the right on an arc at an ascending angle within a second.

After stopping right up there only for a split second, the thing swung all the way to the left on an arc at an acute ascending angle within one second also to be stopped there for the last time for only a split second before launching its final zapping away into the blue sky to be disappeared from my eyesight very swiftly. Once and for all, the thing had to expose a full range of its zigzag maneuver from start to end.

In fact, I happened to see the whole departure mode from a zero speed to a wild speed. It was just like watching a spontaneous drag race on the street, in which a car would accelerate from a standstill to a full-blown speed in seconds. In essence, the thing could disappear from my eyesight in a hurry by making only 4 swings on 4 arcs within less than 8 seconds in all before gaining its full speed. It was shocking.

To this day, I vividly remember factual elements of the zigzag flight path that I was somehow fortunate enough to observe all the details in its entirety. As I recall, the first arc to the left from a dead center in the sky was the shortest with about 300 feet long. The second arc to the far right or the third arc to the far left was about 600 or 1,200 feet long, respectively. The fourth arc to the far right was the longest.

Now, I would like to describe the thing's flight path in terms of its pretty distinctive sharp angle which I cannot forget for the rest of my life. During its shocking departure mode, it changed its direction of travel to the opposite way three times at an acute ascending angle of about 30 degrees while going up and up and up and up each time. It reached a considerable height with only 3 turning points in 4 swings.

Concluding from what I followed with my own eyes in broad daylight, a zigzag flight path technology including a stunning corner-turning technique seemed fairly common in the universe and, again, looked very simple. Who knows? It might be a matter of time to solve such a scientific puzzle by thinking deep, different or even illogical outside the box. A 3-D video clip of its movement has been implanted in me.

By the way, the best time to take a detailed look at a certain object is when it is not moving, shaking or spinning. This is part of the factual reason why I was able to observe the gigantic thing in such an eye-popping detail. Due to the same reason, I was also able to observe a top portion of the round thing, which was previously hidden from my vantage point. My chance to do so opened up at all the swing stops.

At the end of each swing on an arc up in the sky, the thing maintained a slanted position with a slight downward angle for a split second. So, for the first time, I was able to observe the top half portion of the gigantic round thing. As expected, I also noticed there a huge dome with a right side up. It was of the same size and covered with the same skin materials, but I happened to spot a rather serious difference.

To my pleasant surprise, just above the bottom edge of the round wall for the huge top dome and a little above a narrow strip of a circular wing protruding out of the sphere, I quickly saw quite a number of small rectangular windows with slightly rounded four corners at regular intervals. The windows looked exactly the same as the ones found on both sides of a passenger airplane flown everywhere on the earth.

FIVE:

I Saw a Gigantic UFO (3)

The whole encounter was a complete shocker to me. However, except on the streets of the hi-tech Silicon Valley, where else should you watch such a hi-tech extraterrestrial performance? Till then, I had not witnessed anything like it. I was under a constant awe during the amazing aerial show. Afterwards, I was dumbfounded for a long time at the place. Then, slowly, real slowly, my internal wheel started to turn to figure out what the gigantic thing was. Back then, I had no way of realizing that I was to learn the whole big picture in bizarre, strange or weird ways and convey it to all others.

During a brief time period of my encounter with the gigantic thing right next to the railroad track near the small intersection in San Jose, California, my body and soul were not working properly due to getting virtually frozen despite I was fully conscious, of course. Nevertheless, I could still pick up in effect all the ins and outs of the thing with a help of my animalistic instinct operating on a subconscious level.

I would like to revisit the familiar-looking windows. I could not and definitely did not count all the windows in a stroke since my vantage point would not allow me to do so. However, per my rough estimate from a recollection, it had maybe a couple of hundred small windows on a single row around its round body right above a protruded circular wing attached to the middle section of the gigantic sphere object.

Each window looked about one and a half feet wide and two feet tall since its height was certainly a little longer than its width according to my lasting memory. In addition to the slightly rounded four corners as mentioned before, all the edge going around a window was finished with a single piece of black-colored rubberlike materials based upon my careful observation if my memory serves correct to this day.

All the windows were identical in shape and size as well. However, I was not able to look inside through them in order to see whether there were any crew and passengers on board since they looked very dark probably due to being tinted heavily or maintaining its cabin lights turned off. At any rate, it was obvious that each window should have been transparent so that any riders could look out of the windows.

I often drive by a strange-looking concrete building with practically no installed windows here in Silicon Valley. The big monotonous building was originally constructed as such by design just because it was to be utilized as a server farm occupied by computers, not humans. Computers have no eyes to look out. There is no need for building windows. For the same exact reason, earthly drones have no windows.

Based on the above cool rationale, let's contemplate the thing logically. Since it certainly had so many windows, it was logical to assume that there had to be some crew and passengers with two big eyes to see. It was not far-fetched. It should make sense to everybody with common sense. As such, I have sensed all this time that the thing was occupied. However, as stressed before, I did not witness actual riders.

According to my impression, a position of windows was quite a bit, i.e., at least about one foot or so, lower than usual if the level of the cabin floor inside could be assumed about the same as the level of the thin circular wing outside. It means that the riders on board could have been quite a bit shorter than the humans. In its departure mode, through the windows, they could have spotted me looking up like a dolt.

Based on my logic, I've been firmly convinced that the supreme beings had to be onboard the thing on that day. Of course, at the scene of the encounter as well as for about 22 years since then, I had not had the foggiest idea on what they were actually doing while quietly floating up in the air. No matter what, I had never been capable of figuring out on the whole big picture myself until I got enlightened in 2006.

At this point, I would like to go back to the amazing zigzag departure mode in order to highlight a few analytical aspects for your understanding. For this, I need to take out certain subliminal details dormant in my long-term memory. Come to think of it, by flying away in such a fashion in the three-dimensional space, the thing was capable of acquiring a tremendous level of acceleration with a fierce momentum.

According to what I saw up-close with my two eyes, it only took the thing less than 8 seconds in all to disappear. Let's analyze the first swing to the far left from a stationary position. Because the thing moved about 300 feet on an arc in 1 second, it was flying at 205 miles per hour. How about the second arc of about 600 feet in length flown in 1 second? Its speed was instantly doubled up to be 410 miles per hour.

How about the third arc? Because the thing moved about 1,200 feet in 1 second also, its speed was now around 820 miles per hour. Then, how about the fourth arc? Even though I was not able to observe to the end of the fourth arc mainly because the thing was already flying too fast for my eyes to catch a glimpse of it and out of my eyesight by then, its speed should have been easily over 1,640 miles per hour.

What do all these mesmerizing performance results mean? A peculiar aspect of the zigzag flight path could be derived from the above observation. In the same amount of time, the thing was easily doubling up its travel distance on its subsequent arc one after another until it perhaps reached a full-blown speed of about 3,000 miles per hour in as well as near the earth atmosphere, which I would elaborate later.

Now, I would focus upon another peculiar aspect of the zigzag flight path. According to what I observed at the time, as described before, the thing kept on going up and up and up and up at a seemingly-fixed sharp angle of about 30 degrees each whenever it stopped to change its direction of travel. Why was an angle of ascent set at about 30 degrees? After pondering for a while, I should dare to say – why not?

Per common sense, a slanted or sloped ascent seems far easier than a vertical ascent. For example, after 19 days of grueling ascending on a huge 3,000-foot vertical granite rock called El Capitan stood inside Yosemite National Park in California, Kevin Jorgeson and Tommy Caldwell finally became the first climbers to complete a historic free ascent on the Dawn Wall on January 15, 2015. It looked real hard.

However, if they had decided to use a long winding trail on a constant slope to get to the top of El Capitan rock, it should have been a cinch accomplished in less than a day. For another example, it takes a power of multiple rockets to launch a space shuttle at a vertical angle, but it takes only a regular jet power for a jumbo aircraft to take off at a slanted or sloped angle which is curiously about 30 degrees as well.

At this time, I would present a flight path simulation. We use a drone designed (i) to fly at a maximum 30-degree angle up or down and (ii) to stop at any aerial spot abruptly before changing a course of travel drastically into any open direction in the air to avoid hitting any wall of the confined facility like a basketball gymnasium. Let's set (D)eparture and (A)rrival spots both on the (C)eiling and on the (F)loor.

The first flight from DF to AF should never have to resort to (ii) as well since it could set its precise direction of travel prior to a takeoff. The second flight from DC to AC should never differ from the first requiring only (i), not (ii). However, due to an altitude gap between two spots traveled, the third flight from DF to AC or the fourth flight from DC to AF should theoretically have to resort to both (i) and (ii).

As you could see from the simulation for a potential flight path of any flying objects for that matter, evidentially a zigzag flying technique seems to be most effective for an interplanetary space travel. Especially where there's a need to offset a planetary gravity such as in the earth atmosphere, the zigzag flight method should prove to be quite ideal for a departure or arrival mode. It looks like a matter of physics.

For example, if we would set up an assumption that the earth isn't round but flat, the shortest distance from San Francisco to Seoul should be on a straight line because both cities are on the same plain on a two-dimensional map. On the other hand, the shortest distance from a certain planet to the earth should be on a straight but vertical line, allowing a zigzag flight to be most useful in a three-dimensional space.

Going back to the thing itself, its body was not built to be directional like any airplane with a nose, fuselage, and tail, but constructed to be non-directional in a sphere shape. As a result, the thing wouldn't have to lose any momentum by trying to align the body with a newly-changed direction of travel while turning a corner even at such an acute angle. In addition, the thing could fly backwards or sideways, too.

As mentioned before, even during the unique zigzag departure mode, the thing was not spinning or turning at all. As such, I really had a plenty of time to observe all kinds of details on the thing itself including its domes, lights, panels, rivets, windows, etc. in a close distance especially in broad daylight. During the awesome encounter, I was also able to notice a strange aspect due to a rather conspicuous absence.

Oddly enough, there were no identifying markers on the thing. I could not see any letters, markings, numbers or symbols in any languages on all the surfaces of the wing or domes. Such an absence should have normally provoked a little fear in me, but I did not even have time for that. All I sensed instantly was that it was not from this world. In fact, the supreme beings rely on no spoken or written languages.

Now, I should talk about one of the most surprising aspects of the thing itself. Contrary to our mundane human expectation, it appeared strikingly frugal as such that it was not even painted. It even looked clumsy, fragile, and tacky. Perhaps it was built in a pragmatic way stressing substance over form. What was important is that it could still afford a safe space travel even in such a worrisome state to my eyes.

At one point in time, I happened to rather think of it as a piece of gigantic toy or one of those fun rides available in a nearby amusement park, but I erased such an idea once I realized that a fun ride would not be able to float by itself. At any rate, the gigantic thing must've come from a distant planet where the supreme beings should make objects with their own hands while not wasting natural resources limited.

Even after the gigantic thing disappeared, I was still frozen in extreme confusion for a long time at the very spot as though I had been struck by a huge lightning in the field. I realized finally that I had been visited by something out of this world briefly. I found myself falling into a primal fear with cold sweat on my back. Soon, I could calm down a bit once I did observe a whole bunch of other cars on the street.

Gradually, step by step, my curiosity was narrowed down to determining the nature of it. I began to ask myself stupid questions. What was it? Was it an airplane? No, an airplane can't stop in the air. Was it a helicopter, then? No, it was gigantic, dead quiet with no rotating blades. Was it a flying saucer? Yes, it must have been a UFO. Oh, my god! Finally at that moment, I realized what the thing really was.

Later on, as I was fully regaining myself, I started to look around the place rather carefully. The sun was still up. It was above the horizon, getting ready to go down. All the pilots passing in the sky were perhaps busy communicating with the air traffic controllers for landing at the airport. All the drivers were still crawling in a heavy traffic jam behind enormous walnut trees along the road. I was still by myself.

Unfortunately, there was nobody else other than me on the ground where such an overwhelming extraterrestrial event was witnessed. To my disappointment, I did not even have a camera with me to take a picture. All other personal imagery recording devices like a camcorder, digital camera or smartphone were not even heard of back then. Therefore, I could only record a detailed account with utmost sincerity.

SIX:

A Mature Soul's Journey

Throughout your life on the earth, your soul gets to interact with endless other souls of different maturity levels. Some souls are fully mature already while all the others are in a wide range of maturity in progress. At the end of each life cycle, what happens to a still immature soul? It gets to be reincarnated eventually into a brand-new body and goes through another mode of getting more mature in a new life. Furthermore, what happens to an already fully mature soul? It gets to take a sudden journey with the supreme beings to their own world. I happened to meet one on such a journey.

Once I go to bed at night, I don't normally wake up in the middle and stay awake for long. However, for some reason, I went astray from my nightly routine on November 24, 2004. I happened to wake up at 3:00 a.m. and engaged in thinking about all sorts of daily matters in the bed for an hour with eyes wide-open toward the dark slanted bedroom ceiling. It was weird that I could not go back to sleep at all.

As usual, it was a quiet night as if I could even hear a pin drop. According to my Casio digital watch on my left wrist, on which I checked the time in darkness by pushing a tiny light button, it just turned precisely 4:00 a.m. Right at that moment, another strange event began to unfold in front of my own ears and eyes. Swiftly, I took in a female voice calling my uniquely-familiar Korean home name Dae Yoon.

In fact, I heard it pretty loud and clear. Immediately, I knew whose voice it was. It was certainly the voice of my aunt, but she was supposed to live in South Korea, not here in America. As such, I got terribly confused rather quickly. In order to control my sanity, I decided not to trust my ears and did not budge. Besides, I was too surprised to respond. Hence, I pretended that I simply misheard the whole sound.

Several seconds passed. The voice called me again for the second time. I turned my head a little bit to the right since the voice surely came from my right-hand side where there existed a modest walk space on the floor between the queen-sized bed and a set of big sliding glass doors leading to an atrium in the middle of our single-story four-bedroom small house situated on the outskirts of San Jose, California.

Right away, I was shocked to discover that my aunt was standing close to me in a lovely ambient white Korean traditional dress. I paid my attention to her glistening eyes. While we interchanged a direct eye contact with each other, she called me yet again for the third time with a marvelous smile. She truly looked sharp and vivid under a bright spot light as if she was performing on stage in a Broadway play.

Of course, I was way more than glad to see her, but I could not physically respond at all for a rather long period of time to me. I was directly looking up at her up-close and hearing her loud and clear voice to call me again and again, but I could never even budge any part of my body, let alone responding to repeated callings from my aunt, because I got instantly frozen as soon as I found her in our own bedroom.

A biting moment of total silence descended upon us while calmly looking at each other rather intently. Actually, I was eying to read her wide-open eyes filled with a special feeling of care and love because I knew that she was trying to give me a message through her eyes. Her eyes made me understand that she was on her way to go to a remote place. Amazingly, she was communicating with me telepathically.

Soon after, she again called my name loud and clear for the fourth time without losing her constant lovely smile. At that moment, I suddenly realized that she could really go away from me forever any moment. So, I erected my upper body, turned right to sit on the edge, and extended my right arm straight toward her in order to grab her right wrist area. I thought I actually touched her right forearm. It was not so.

Certainly, aiming was perfect on my part. I did not even blink my eyes at the time. However, to my surprise, I ended up holding nothing with my hand, for she completely disappeared like a puff of smoke in less than a split second as the bright spot light got turned off by someone somehow. I was totally shocked at the sudden encounter with my aunt. The whole fascinating event lasted over 20 seconds for sure.

If an extremely extraordinary incident occurs to you especially when you're least expecting or prepared, you get confused and you try to figure it out yourself. I did just that. My wife was still in a quite deep sleep to my left in the bed. Though it was tempting, I didn't bother to wake her up just to tell her something that I couldn't even fully comprehend. As such, I ended up struggling alone in darkness to no avail.

In the morning, I told her what had happened to me during the night. She took it as something unreal, but had a hunch that something bad might have happened to my aunt in Seoul, Korea. She insisted me to place a call right away, but I could not locate her phone number for a sloppy reason. I kept searching for a small piece of scratch paper on which I would have written down her apartment telephone number.

Regretfully, a little over two months passed by with no further action on my part to inquire about her well-being. The only reminder for the whole event was a small graphic note that I left on a wall calendar hung in our bedroom. On January 27, 2005, I got a sad e-mail with an apology for not informing me earlier. It was from a nephew in South Korea. Per him, she passed away precisely on November 24, 2004.

Immediately, I examined the November page of the old calendar. Lo and behold, as expected, the small graphic mark depicting my actual encounter with her was located in the blank square designated for November 24, 2004. Wow! Asking for more details such as the exact time of her death, I e-mailed him right back. According to his reply received, she died of old age on a hospital bed over there at 5:00 p.m.

A gut feeling hit my curiosity. From it, I subtracted 17 hours for time difference between San Jose and Seoul to confirm my instinct. Per Pacific Standard Time, she ebbed away there at midnight and came here to see me at 4:00 a.m. on the same November 24, 2004. Factually, wow, her soul traveled approximately 6,000 miles from Seoul to San Jose all within exactly 4 hours after it came out of her dead body.

Did I see her ghost? No, definitely not. I still don't think so. Based upon what I have picked up from others in my life so far or as far as I know, a ghost cannot portray an alert, clear, crisp, lively, shiny, and vivid presence for itself. Absolutely, when I saw my aunt in the middle of that night, I clearly thought that a real live person came over to see me. The fact that I tried to hold her with my hand proves a point.

As such, at the time, I was not afraid to see her at all. Moreover, even to this day, I get to picture her lovely smile whenever I happen to think of the whole event from time to time. For close to two years afterwards until I got suddenly enlightened in 2006 or even a lot longer, I had been kept in the dark as to how or why the final encounter with my aunt took place. I would convey you step by step what I learned.

In a humongous pile of the enlightenment materials given to me on July 7, 2006, there existed also a fascinating piece of knowledge that could provide a theoretical basis to explain nearly all the ins and outs as to how or why such an encounter with my aunt took place as if in a great fairy tale. Upon passing away, her soul slipped out of her body, arose above her, and wandered around in the air for about an hour.

When the time came, a visiting UFO showed up and picked up her soul along with other souls floating in the sky. Soon after, her soul was lined up in an orderly process for a comprehensive and cumulative maturity test carried out by the supreme beings. Basically, her entire life history was to be reviewed by them to determine her soul's maturity level. Her soul turned out to be fully mature according to a result.

Based on a meticulous review process, she was told that she would be taken away from the earth to their planet in order to start an eternal life as one of the supreme beings. Without hesitation, she appealed to them that she really had to see one of her kids living in San Jose, California, for the last time before being escorted away from the earth forever. Her appeal got accepted only after checking all the logistics.

In actuality, after spending an hour aboard the UFO, her soul was at last on her way to crop up in front of me by flying over the vast Pacific Ocean with the supreme beings. It took them 2 hours to travel a whopping distance of about 6,000 miles at an impressive speed of 3,000 miles per hour. Indisputably, it provided me with clear factual evidence on a full-blown speed of a UFO flying in the earth atmosphere.

In fact, no earthly public transport devices available could cover 6,000 miles in 2 hours, but the whole encounter with her soul was possible due to the amazing assistance by the supreme beings. In approving her personal appeal to do so, they had to assess upfront all the logistics involving me and my surroundings as well so as to guarantee a successful extraterrestrial mission on the spot even without rehearsing.

Obviously, they had to study beforehand whom she wanted to meet with, where I was to be located on the earth, what I was doing at the time, how my house was positioned, in which room and on which side of the bed I was sleeping, and which spot of the bedroom was suited for me to see her life-sized 3-D figure or hologram in color without blockage. The last element was crucial because she was 63 inches tall.

As a matter of fact, they also had to study obviously whether the left sliding door of the 78-inch-tall glass doors had its drapes fully open so that they could do a job without a hitch as well as whether I would be totally awake with my eyes wide-open at the very moment of upcoming encounter. Pertaining to the latter, it seemed reasonable to assume that they could have even made me wake up to wait for my aunt.

In other words, only after securing a workable space in terms of direct access, projecting angle, visible spot, etc., they decided to proceed with the sophisticated performance across the vast ocean. However, I was still kept in the dark as to the actual techniques involved for a long time to come. A final clue on how they actually pulled it off was given to me on November 21, 2014, which I would convey you later.

Now, I would like to talk about my aunt. Her name was Jung Soon Shin. Her soul was beautiful, brave, caring, conscientious, considerate, fair, friendly, generous, genuine, honest, kind, lovely, open, polite, righteous, smart, straight, warm, wise, and above all extremely mature. She was born to a rich family of the very first gold store in Korea, but she had no formal education per customs not to educate women.

Most of her life, she lived hopelessly dirt poor since her husband was a moneyless countryman and he died early. Yet, with love, she raised me like her own son for 13 years. To me, with a strong emotional tie, she is my mother per se. She always taught herself and taught me a lot about life, too. "To a person you resent, serve one more piece of rice cake," she often said, reminding me not to make an enemy in mind.

In a favela of Seoul, when I was about ten years old, I happened to behave a little rude to others. She took me to a nearby mountaintop and told me to collect some switches to my surprise. I thought she would hit me with them later. So, I got only soft ones. Instead, I had to find real switches. However, she never hit me even when she was supposed to. She only whipped her own legs for failing to teach me right.

On November 24, 1994, I visited my native land for the first time in 18 years. The first thing I did in Seoul was to literally look for my aunt. Finally, I heard her voice on a phone. She called my home name exactly 4 times. I could not even open my mouth. Eventually, a friend of mine took over the phone. I was frozen just like exactly 10 years later on November 24, 2004. Honestly, was it just a coincidence?

SEVEN:
How to Get More Mature

Stay calm and look around. You would readily find that everybody has a uniquely different set of body and soul. Even within the same sex, no two bodies or souls should be exactly the same even if they are identical twins. In fact, all the human beings are different from one another in terms of body and soul. For our discussion, let's focus on their soul. A maturity of each and every soul fluctuates throughout life. At every moment in life, a soul may pass through a different part of a maturity scale with marks of 0 to 100 for instance. How could a person reach a better part of a maturity scale?

For a close examination, let me recite those 20 good characters of my aunt's soul such as beautiful, brave, caring, conscientious, considerate, fair, friendly, generous, genuine, honest, kind, lovely, open, polite, righteous, smart, straight, warm, wise, and above all extremely mature. Interestingly, a virtue of being mature is undoubtedly most critical simply because it serves as a solid basis for all the other characters.

Oh, no other virtue can do it easily for all the others. How mesmerizing the point is! Some may pick conscience for the role, but it does not fit, for it can be system-sensitive. Of course, countless other good characters can also be cited on a soul. However, you would soon realize that a virtue of maturity permeates through most likely all the other virtues. It surely means that, lacking maturity, there is no good soul.

It also means that a virtue of maturity would contain within itself any other good virtues present in a typical soul. In other words, once a soul is measured to be at the highest level of a maturity scale, all the other aspects of such a soul could be overlooked quite safely. This is precisely why the supreme beings would concentrate by design all their effort into examining a soul's maturity level when the time comes.

Realistically, how would they go about examining it? When they would visit a soul farm and pick up a ready soul for an exam of maturity, they would conduct a maturity test while reviewing a just-finished life history of it under exam. For a reason unknown to me back then, the supreme beings sent me the one and only maturity test around 6:36 a.m. on April 5, 2014. It seems to be so simple to anyone's surprise.

The maturity test revolves around only one question: Except in a situation where you personally had to carry out a certain thing entirely against your own free will, have you ever caused a damage in any way, shape or form to another person or another group in order to advance or protect your own or group's interest in any way, shape or form by taking advantage of the situation no matter what, when, and where?

It is a kind of negative test. 'Yes' fails. 'No' passes. It can also be shortened: Have you stepped on top of others? It's that simple, wow! However, if you think about it deep, it is not quite simple. In fact, it is a very tall order imposed on the human beings by the supreme beings with a purpose of assuring to harvest only fully mature souls as efficiently as possible after creating, bringing, inserting, nurturing, etc.

For all practical purposes, their role in dealing with all the human beings on the earth and in the whole universe for that matter is quite similar to a typical orchard farmer's. It seems intriguing. For your understanding, I would like to give you a personal story. In our little backyard, I planted a dwarf orange tree myself. After nurturing and watering for many years, I was able to enjoy quite a few savory oranges.

From my perspective, they are like my own children. I'd never harm the oranges except by eventual consumption which is all right since their only purpose of existing on the earth by intention from the supreme beings is to nourish the human beings or any others in need. In terms of harvesting, I wouldn't even pick them off the tree unless I truly have to. I would rather pick them up under the tree after being fallen.

Conclusively by the same token, the supreme beings would not harm or kill any human beings on their soul farm prematurely. They possess no incentive. Look for the past such history, or lack of it. They don't even deface nature as evidenced in crop circles. After all, we would dedicate our precious life to mature their souls so that they could harvest when the time comes. It is to their advantage not to hurt us.

Accordingly, we should not fear the supreme beings. Instead, we should do our best in cooperating with them for their legitimate efforts to successfully produce a designated quantity of fully mature souls for use as quickly as possible. In fact, this is an astonishingly pragmatic core concept that could assist both the supreme beings and the human beings greatly if and only if it gets to be known to the entire globe.

However, two-way communication channels for the supreme and human beings could only be used case by case. They are not for mass communications. In order to resolve a dilemma, the supreme beings perhaps could have decided to communicate to me individually so that I might do a job of making humans aware of the whole big picture for them. I could be wrong on this, but I could be right on this as well.

At this point, I would convey you a word of caution that they would never expect us to lead a perfect life all the time on the earth because they themselves could never even do so all the time on their own planets. Only all the gods in our human souls can be assumed to do so. All the physical beings in the universe are in the same boat making mistakes. As such, let us not despair even if we are not always perfect.

What's really important would not be what we were, but what we are and could be. Only if your soul contains a consistent improvement or tendency toward achieving such a lofty goal, it would be considered as getting more mature. This is part of the reason why they would only review your just-finished life history when the time comes. They hardly care about prior life histories archived within the same soul.

As you know, virtually everybody cannot remember any details on his or her early life before 3 or 4 years of age, let alone such details on preceding life or lives if any. Why? It is because our human brain with a limited capacity would be quite busy in the early years reorganizing, i.e., archiving a prior life history at the end of already-archived ones while developing, in order to make room for usage in current life.

As a result, under a special type of hypnosis to find out anything on a prior life, most people could only recall a death scene of their last prior life. Meanwhile, the supreme beings would rarely bother to review any prior life histories stored in an archive format in a corner of a soul under exam. Then, what would be a use for keeping them in a soul at all? They shall be used in an eternal life if everything goes right.

It works like this. If and when your own soul would be fully mature already in current or subsequently in future life after being reincarnated once or more depending on the outcome of each successive life cycle and would be able to lead an eternal life at last as one of the supreme beings on a distant planet in the universe, you would have to draw from your own cumulative life experience extracted for reference.

As a matter of the universe, such a planet is just like a heavenly paradise or an imaginary place such as so-called Shangri-La or Utopia where the supreme beings would lead an eternal life in supreme happiness without a single fear of being harmed in any way, shape or form by all kinds of bad episodes like crimes, deaths, diseases, fights, killings, wars, etc. However, an only exception would be natural disasters.

On such a planet, there should be no need to employ any attorneys, doctors, guards, officers, politicians, soldiers, etc. As a consequence, there should be no need to establish courts, governments, hospitals, laws, prisons, weapons, etc. Based on the above factors, there should be no need to have countries with borders, either. Now, could you see why the supreme beings would need to have fully mature souls only?

What if the supreme beings would permit immature souls to be utilized in brand-new members of their societies? Without even thinking, you should know the correct answer. Each and every heavenly place would turn into a chaos or a mess just like one of their soul farms – the earth. Now, you should totally comprehend the one and only reason why the earth is always in dire straits. Unfortunately, it is by design.

No matter how many previous life cycles they went through on the earth, all the current souls began with a zero maturity initially after being manufactured, transported, and inserted into respective new bodies to be born at a different point in time. Also, each and every soul could pass through various parts of a maturity scale at any point throughout life. That's precisely why you could see diverse levels of people.

All souls at first were blank, empty or even identical with no content except for a generic perfect god embedded. Nevertheless, they were not even informed of their purpose of existence on the earth, let alone the whole big picture for which they shall function at all. Hence, people rarely even know what a real job in life should be. It is like a situation lacking a GPS navigator or a map. We're bound to get lost.

If lost, we become confused, get into any directions, and most likely waste our time wandering around anywhere and everywhere doing all sorts of good things or bad things. This neat logic should explain why the world appears to be full of good people as well as bad people at any moment in time. However, in real life, no one is always either good or bad continually from birth to death. We all have both sides.

In the meantime, when we do an exceptionally good thing or bad thing, we know upfront what we will really do deep down in our soul. We tend to look around beforehand. All these complex behavior patterns would culminate quite heavily in satisfying a basic notion that we are not meant to be perfect at all mainly because we could always learn from bad as well as good things to mature our soul a little deeper.

However, if interested, please peruse any newspaper, identify responsible parties for positive or negative articles, and speculate their respective maturity level while keeping tab on mature vs. immature souls. I did it in February 2015. Though unscientific, world-wide news briefs on the front of the Wall Street Journal produced an average of 9% vs. 91%. It is too lopsided. The earth suffers a serious problem to fix.

In living our life as a whole on the earth, we are into so many wrong directions. As such, the supreme beings are worried about us because they have the most at stake in our souls. Although we're extremely effective in disseminating information through a worldwide use of high-speed Internet, we must be getting gradually away from maturing our souls, for we do not know exactly what to do, how to do, and why.

Hopefully, by now, in full, I have explained and you have understood with regard to a subject of maturing a soul. At this point, aside from my one and only aunt, I would like to introduce another person with a fully mature soul, whom I was quite fortunate to be associated with in my teen years. He was a very close friend of mine at a school in Seoul and his name was In Myung Yang. I heard he passed away, too.

Whenever I met him by chance waiting at a bus stop, I happened to get to school late in the morning just because he refused to get on any crowded bus no matter how long it might take to spot a less crowded bus and I refused to leave him behind although I never asked him why he was so odd. Only last year, I realized that he behaved uniquely since he did not want to step on top of others by invading their space.

Of course, I should not be the only human being on the earth, whom the supreme beings have kind of attempted to engage in order to convey their extraterrestrial messages on what they really want from us. Only after realizing their practical dilemma and urgent request by putting together all the puzzle pieces that I happened to possess, I have decided to cooperate with them. In actuality, it should only help us.

EIGHT:

Facts on Soul vs. Spirit (1)

Surely, soul is to spirit as operating system software is to application software. For three long days, my thought on soul vs. spirit could not move any further from the above. Word lookups in many dictionaries were not much of a help. Google searches on the subject added even more confusion. However, on the fourth day, the supreme beings stepped in and made me grasp the whole nine yards to share with you. For real, aside from the human beings, could you name any other earthly species with a full range of facial expressions? No, definitely not. Strange, isn't it? Let's solve the mystery.

Have you seen a dead person, i.e., a body without a soul, for real? I have. In a way to say goodbye for the last time, I've even kissed a close friend of mine on his ice-cold forehead positioned in a casket. Once his soul left his done body on a patient bed at Stanford Hospital on May 14, 2004, he turned pale in a hurry looking like a piece of plastic doll. Life and death seemed drastically different as day and night.

Just this morning, I was asked to pick up a dead bug from the floor, but I was never certain whether it was really dead or not even after I scooped it up in a small plastic bag mainly because there seemed to be absolutely no difference between life and death with regard to its bodily appearance. Unlike my friend, the dead insect did not need a makeup to look as if being alive. It had no soul to lose. It lost a spirit.

Do you see a dramatic distinction between having a soul or not and having a spirit or not in the above examples? Of course, both soul and spirit should dictate life and death in all the species. Being fundamentally different from spirit, soul seems to dictate our appearance in life or death as well. In a nutshell, our soul is active in our brain behind our face that is our soul's mirror. Facial expressions reflect our soul.

To tell you the truth, I had absolutely no knowledge in depth on a rather complex and extremely delicate subject of facts on soul vs. spirit even when I decided to talk about it just last week. As a result, for the first three days, I could come up with nothing but a single sentence with an analogy to computer software. Besides adding even more confusion, my research effort in dictionaries or Google was to no avail.

While getting into bed at night after three frustrated days, I actually requested the supreme beings calmly in my mind to teach me the whole thing covering a subject of soul vs. spirit. Simply, it was a sincere piece of my own thought in a short English sentence to the supreme beings in charge of my current project that would carry out their own request for conveying all critical core concepts to the human beings.

Normally, I can't and don't remember nearly all my dreams once I get up. Even if I do remember some later on occasionally, my memory won't last long enough to be sure. During the night, I had four dreams. As usual, the first two dreams were immediately forgotten. However, the last two dreams were so unusual that I could never forget about any. In fact, I could and did even realize more vivid details later.

Dream A took place within the exact premise of our current house. Scene 1: When I arrived at home after work, my wife told me from the dark kitchen that she got a phone call from a gentleman representing an association unknown and that he informed her of some sort of construction work to be conducted for free. Scene 2: The doorbell rang once. I opened up the white front door to greet a group of visitors.

I saw a middle-aged gentleman in front of the group, who looked like a foreman, in addition to three other young men in the back, who looked like his crew. They appeared clean, handsome and properly dressed for their line of work. The foreman had a dress shirt with a pair of khaki pants on. All laborers had T-shirts with pants on. Two had blue jeans. However, they just stared at me blankly without any words.

Accordingly, I had to assume myself at the door that they were all from the so-called association and let them in. Scene 3: They took all the furniture out of the corner room where I really happened to sleep for the first time that night. An obnoxious stench had forced me out of the middle room where I stayed having no CPAP machine yet. In the dream, I couldn't figure out where they were stashing the furniture.

They neither talked nor exchanged any hand signals while moving. They all seemed to know exactly what to do. Scene 4: They took down the one and only big rectangular window in the corner room to the middle of the floor. Two laborers set it straight up by firmly grabbing from both ends. The third laborer wiped clean its outer surface with a towel and a bucketful of water. He did it fast in a skilled manner.

Then, with both hands, the foreman put on the glass a sheet of beige wallpaper glued wet. It looked thin, lightly printed with colorful flowers, and opaque to my eyes. Soon, the room became dark because someone turned off the light. Immediately, a rectangular beam of super-bright white light angled into the very hollow opening in the wall to penetrate the decorated windowpane propped up vertical on the floor.

To my pleasant surprise, the covered window was at least semitransparent, not entirely opaque. I saw the whole demonstration. Of course, they performed all of their tasks without a hitch with no word spoken to each other or to me. Scene 5: I was watching network news on TV alone in our master bedroom. When I heard the doorbell ring again, my flat TV screen transitioned from news to guests at our door.

In my dream, I thought it was pretty strange because we had not installed any security cameras at our household. Furthermore, it was also quite strange to spot another group of four men standing outside the door, who looked perhaps exactly the same as the first group of one foreman and three laborers. As I was wondering who opened the door, the left half of the screen employed another camera to show inside.

Oh, it was the very foreman who answered the door. However, instead of letting them in, he tried to signal them to buzz off by giving the other foreman a subtle gesture of a little wink and a fast but limited neck swing to his right. So as to satisfy my curiosity, I again wondered whether it was possible to zoom in on the second foreman's crammed face. To my surprise, the right half of the screen zoomed in close.

Lo and behold, the second foreman's big face in the right half of the screen turned out to be exactly the same as the first foreman's face in the left half of the screen for sure. I was fearfully shocked to confirm that my initial suspicion over their real identities was dead correct. Even in my own dream, I was a genuinely cautious person who would make an actual move only after confirming all the pertinent facts.

Scene 6: Armed with a new revelation based on the incredible facts, I barged out to the hallway to confront him. The foreman quickly turned around toward me immediately after closing the front door on the second foreman and three other young men. I asked him out loud who they were, but he was totally silent with an apparent blank look on his face. I shouted that I saw the whole thing and they were the same.

No matter what, I had to let it out of my own system although I sensed that he would neither react nor respond in any way, shape or form to my genuine outcry. As expected, the foreman never spilled a word through his zipped mouth. He never showed any facial expressions whatsoever, either. In fact, all the other seven men who actually participated in my dream were also entirely speechless and expressionless.

Due to frustration and a primal fear of the unknown, I wanted to get out of the Dream A quickly. Abruptly, I did. It was 6:00 a.m. when I woke up. Except going over to the restroom briefly to release, I remained wide-awake alone in the bed for an hour. I was wary a little with fear and jitters provoked by a vivid remembrance of the grotesque content. I was puzzled as well. It was Sunday on February 15, 2015.

Soon after, I found myself within Dream B that was taking place on one of the sunny boulevards in Los Angeles. Scene 1: After meeting with a lady pertaining to one of the cases that I was working on, I just came out of her house to the street, but I simply could not find my car in the vicinity. I sensed vaguely that perhaps I never even drove a car there since I could not even remember parking any car in the area.

Scene 2: When I was about to phone home with my iPhone to find out whether or not my car was actually there, I was swiftly confronted by two male muggers asking me to hand over my invaluable smartphone. When I refused their unlawful request by shouting that I could not do so because it was very important to me, they both threatened me with a sharp eight-inch single-edged knife in their respective hand.

Scene 3: Immediately, I took out my own knife, too, which happened to be astonishingly identical to their knives, and grabbed it with my right hand in a defensive mode, i.e., a blade portion down. Apparently, it was not good enough. Pretty soon, I had to upgrade my grab to an offensive mode, i.e., a blade portion up, and challenged them for their attack. Scene 4: They talked to each other and started to run away.

I scared them away by demonstrating my own brave attitude of not only defending me but also attacking them if necessary. Afterwards, I opened my eyes. It was 8:00 a.m. In the Dream B, after all, I was most likely James Rockford in the Rockford Files on TV. The late James Garner played a popular private investigator. Actually, a tiny victory gave me a bit of boost. However, the Dream A still bothered me.

For real, I am kind of a little too slow in recognizing a pattern of significance. Only after three more long hours crawled away from me, I definitely realized acutely that the last two dreams were symbolic by nature. It was a result of constant intuitive thinking from outside the box on my part. In those two dreams, all the critical elements prerequisite to understanding facts on soul vs. spirit were sensibly present.

Clearly, they were way more than just being critical. They were factually so concrete, indicative, substantial, and tangible that I could readily scoop up all the key ingredients out of them very smoothly. With all the basics in my hands, nearly any questions with respect to soul vs. spirit could be fully answered accurately at last once and for all. No doubt, the supreme beings gave me the whole thing to disseminate.

From my perspective, I could come up with nothing else than the above observation due to a tenacious series of odd but real phenomenon taken place before and after those two symbolic dreams that I experienced in the corner room. The offensive smell from the middle room ceiling area and the white wooden horizontal Venetian blinds in both rooms contributed heavily to making me experience those dreams.

By meticulously manipulating or steadily increasing a degree of bad odor in the middle room, they forced me to the corner room where it was possible for them to secure an unblocked view of me from their space through directional openings of the blinds so that they could send me telepathic dreams without a hitch. Believe it or not, according to tacit experiments, the above factuality was conclusively the case.

In fact, the smell began on the first day of my whole frustration over soul vs. spirit. It turned stronger every day. It was still utterly horrid around 8:00 a.m. on the fourth day. Upon interpreting those symbolic dreams around 11:00 a.m. while having coffee in the kitchen, I knew behind the scene that it was gone, went to the middle room with my wife and son, and got shocked to confirm its complete disappearance.

In addition to their symbolic answers to teach me on the subject in question, the supreme beings were also trying to give me some important clues with regard to maintaining a suitable environment for sending and receiving telepathic messages to and from them based on a dream content of the so-called construction work. As such, I am planning to tell you the whole nine yards about mechanics of telepathy, too.

NINE:

Facts on Soul vs. Spirit (2)

Only the human beings possess both soul and spirit here on the earth except for the supreme beings visiting the earth soul farm. Other species in animals, insects, monads, and plants do not possess soul. Instead, they possess spirit. All the other physical things as well as all the dead species possess neither one of them. Only the human beings out of all the species cannot survive on spirit alone. If they could, we should call them zombies, defining them as dead people without soul but with spirit to walk around dazed in fiction. In my extraterrestrial dream, I saw 8 such zombies in effect.

As touched upon briefly before, I had my own share of ah-ha moment, i.e., an instantaneous epiphany, regarding the two seemingly-scary but dramatically-symbolic dreams absolutely around 11:00 a.m. on Sunday, February 15, 2015. They were not meant to be casual dreams that I was used to. The fact that I could not and did not forget about any detail with regard to their factual content proves my point for sure.

As you should have noticed easily, perhaps because the supreme beings produced both dreams from outer space, all the dramatic scenes from each dream were so well-made much like Hollywood studio production works. There were factually no holes in their unique story lines, let alone their improbably-complex thus ostensibly-simple extraterrestrial messages with regard to the whole subject of soul vs. spirit.

Well, from a symbolic perspective, let's analyze the Dream A in which two separate but identical groups of four zombies each showed up out of nowhere and did or tried to perform rather sophisticated tasks for the construction work. Oddly enough, they never spoke a word of human language such as English, nor displayed any type of facial expression. Moreover, they didn't even know how to process a thought.

From start to end, they serenely worked and worked. They seemed to do correctly what they were supposed to do. They perhaps never deviated from what they were expected to carry out in terms of all those nitty-gritty duties involved including answering the door, generating covert gestures to alert the foreman of the other team to go away, and so forth. They were not different from animals, insects, monads, etc.

In other words, with regard to all the movements of their factual bodily work, they clearly seemed to follow all predetermined, preprogrammed, and reactionary behavioral patterns with no questions voiced whatsoever. Except for a negligible level of minimal thinking power incorporated as a form of preset bodily movements, they could not exercise the same level of complex brain power of the human beings.

In essence, by dramatically contrasting the zombies to the human beings, the supreme beings were teaching me how to distinguish spirit from soul. Instantly, anyone could pinpoint all four classification criteria in the above analysis, which would include linguistic versatility, facial expression, thinking capability, and bodily movement. Without a doubt, soul dictates the first three factors and spirit dictates the last.

Furthermore, from the same symbolic point of view, let's analyze the Dream B in which three human beings, i.e., two muggers and a target, were involved in a confrontation. Obviously, everyone in a tangle spoke some words out loud, displayed resilient raw emotions through facial expressions, exerted a wild range of thinking capability surrounding any crime and self-defense actions, and conducted actual moves.

As expected, in the above analysis for the Dream B, the first three points were dictated by their soul and the last point was dictated by their spirit. In a nutshell, the supreme beings meticulously engineered another signifying example casting me as the crime target for the muggers to emphasize the fact that the live human beings have both soul and spirit. No doubt, both dreams provided a full sketch of the subject.

Now, let's briefly focus on one of the odd moments in the Scene 5 of the Dream A to think about its hidden but profound implications with respect to the very nature of the supreme beings. It was the scene with the second group of four men featured in front of the door. The association sent them down to follow the first group of four men most likely for the same construction job either by design or by mistake.

Based on my own perspective heavily influenced by an ongoing series of strange or weird extraterrestrial events that I have witnessed consistently here on the earth, I could only come up with my own conjecture that such association introduced as a generic organization should be factually run by the supreme beings on their planet in the universe. Then, what was their actual point with regard to the second group?

In light of what I have learned, obtained or received in numerous occasions, I kind of naturally know already for real the one and only accurate answer to the above question. One way or another, the supreme beings wanted to reiterate that they are not perfect unlike any god created and revered only by the human beings and that they do make occasional mistakes like the human beings since their soul is the same.

Close your eyes and look around. What do you see? Do you see a perfect world? No, definitely not. How come? All the living things including especially the human beings surviving on the earth are imperfect, for the supreme beings are their original creators and they themselves are imperfect in the first place. Imperfect beings create imperfect beings. Open your eyes and look around. Can you see who you are?

Getting back to the subject of facts on soul vs. spirit, the live human beings possess soul, being entirely different from the other species in animals, insects, monads or plants. In contrast, all the live species including the earthly human beings possess spirit. Consequently, only the human beings possess both soul and spirit. However, human spirit is a bit different from all the other spirits within the earth soul farm.

Surprisingly, for a good reason, the supreme beings retain an active control on one of the most critical functions of the human spirit. The supreme beings do not manipulate the same function of all the other existing spirits possessed by animals, insects, monads, and plants because they do not maintain any other means of communication than telepathy. Certainly, in this discussion, the function refers to telepathy.

Aside from dictating all ordinary bodily movements exerted through body parts like bones, muscles, nerves, etc. activated with a timely supply of nutrients and oxygen from a continued stream of blood and other bodily fluids needed, all the spirits alive dictate another critical function in terms of telepathy to provide a two-way communication means to exchange messages with themselves or the supreme beings.

In case of the live human beings with soul and spirit, a complete feature of telepathic function is already installed in a corner of every spirit, except that its reception channel is systematically paused by the supreme beings. How come? It could be counterproductive and dangerous for the human beings to use both fully-functional telepathy and languages, for immature people are bound to abuse them to a detriment.

Accordingly, the supreme beings had no choice but to limit a part of telepathy in order to prevent any confusion, hardship or problem which the human beings might have to endure unnecessarily by using both languages and telepathy. No live beings must utilize both means of communications. Meantime, its transmission channel of the human telepathy is not even equipped with a pause button for a good reason.

What about the supreme beings who possess a fully mature soul? Do they have both means? Yes. Do they use both means? Yes or no, it depends. What's really going on? For real, they have both linguistic capability and telepathic capability mainly because they possess both soul and spirit. However, they rarely use the former since the latter is more comprehensive. Relying on both can be counterproductive.

Certainly, the above analysis on telepathy illustrates why I was able to send or receive telepathic messages to or from the supreme beings regarding the confusing subject of soul vs. spirit on a real-time basis. In order to keep an open communications channel between us for the current project, the supreme beings have been deactivating the pause button originally installed on my spirit whenever required to do so.

As far as I could learn, there seems to be a lot more purely mechanical elements present in the area of telepathic communication means. As I mentioned previously, I would tell the whole nine yards on telepathy when the time comes. Based upon my own seemingly-ongoing factual experience in exchanging many sophisticated telepathic messages with the supreme beings, it appears to be far more than amazing.

Come to think of it, there was a reason why I had to send the telepathic message to the supreme beings for their assistance on this very complicated subject of soul vs. spirit. When I got enlightened in 2006 from the whole big picture with the universal life system operation rules, I received the telepathic mail with an incredible volume full of fascinating information, but I could not find much information on spirit.

On the contrary, I could easily find all sorts of other incredible information, for instance, about soul. As I recall, it even talked about sex of soul combined with sex of body. Our body has two opposite sex types, i.e., female and male. By the same token, nearly all the other species found on the earth also enjoy the same bodily makeup as usual in nature. It appears to be quite consistent with only minor exceptions.

For now, let's focus our discussion on sex of human soul so as to probe its relationship with sex of human body. As you must have learned on your own throughout your life, according to what the supreme beings conveyed over to me, our soul also has the same opposite sex types as female and male. Further, sex of our soul could never be changed once they tear off a brand-new unisex soul into two pieces to use.

By design, a human soul shows no racial distinction, meaning that it is inserted into a body across different races. However, their insertion work takes place too early before a sex of an embryo or fetus can be easily identified. Actually, the supreme beings possess an imperfect but intelligent soul. By chance or design, off and on, they would insert a female soul into a male body or put a male soul into a female body.

The former makes a gay man and the latter a lesbian. Naturally, it is simply a biological transgender case to them. From the moment of birth, their own soul should feel quite awkward or uncomfortable with their own given body since they absolutely do not match each other. As a consequence, they would have no choice but to feel a sexual attraction to a person of the same sex with their own given body, period.

Further, some biologically-homosexual people may go an extra step to adopt a drastic measure and change their body into the opposite sex, thereby becoming a transsexual in order to achieve conformity between their body and soul. A choice of surgery or therapy may look drastic, but it must be understandable due to no chance of converting their soul. Even so, would it be wise if one was born as such by design?

In the meanwhile, a feeling of love dictates a sexual attraction while a human soul dictates both. A human body is nothing but a mechanical tool that supports a human soul. As such, our soul precedes our body in exerting preference. For this reason, with regard to love or sexuality, the human beings should be attracted to each other primarily based on the sex of their soul, not the sex of their body, in most cases.

Equipped with all these universal biological facts on our human sexuality, general population in any homosexual community or any heterosexual society for that matter must feel comfortable and natural about themselves or any others. After all, the whole setup is based on yin and yang biology, and nobody seems to go against nature if you look carefully. In fact, no core concepts introduced so far go against nature.

TEN:

Mechanics of Telepathy (1)

If you pick up its whole mechanics, you will see that telepathy is of course neither paranormal nor supernatural. It is simply a communication means for all the spirits in the universe. Since all the human beings have spirit as well as soul, we have it as well. Nonetheless, we could only send it. We could never receive it unless the supreme beings would deactivate a pause button for a reason whenever necessary. As a result, most people don't even know we have it as well. In fact, praying is an act of sending a telepathic message to the supreme beings. It has nothing to do with any religions.

On the earth alone, so many different languages are being used, but only the human beings use them as a means of communications among themselves in certain respective communities, countries or regions through auxiliary means of messages such as book, computer, mail, meeting, movie, newspaper, paper, phone, radio, smartphone, television, etc. in order to hear, listen, read, see, speak, talk, type and write.

On the earth, are there any other living things which use spoken or written languages as a communication means? No, absolutely not. Why not? All those other living things such as animals, insects, monads or plants possess no souls, thus no languages. Instead, each and every one of them has a spirit. As a result, their only means of communications is telepathy amongst themselves and with the supreme beings.

In other words, the supreme beings always maintain a constant two-way telepathic communication channel open with all those other living things on the earth partly because they have originally created every single species of animals, insects, monads, and plants and brought them to the earth in order to make up a beautiful, comfortable, interesting, neat, self-sufficient, and suitable soul farm for the human beings.

As you would know by now, the supreme beings do possess both a soul and a spirit in their distinctively unique respective body pragmatically designed to withstand any of their interplanetary space journeys and diverging planetary conditions where they should reside. For your information, although their souls have two different versions, i.e., female or male, their bodies have only a single version for all souls.

In their quasi-celibate society, there is no such thing as bodily love or physical sex, thereby residing with a zero chance of their eternal life becoming as complicated as ours between men and women along with any children produced. They have mental, profound, thrilling, and timeless platonic love only between two soul mates. Think about our reality. Post-sex love seems downhill, for sex conceives headaches.

In fact, pre-sex love feels sweeter than post-sex love. Now, why would the supreme beings utilize only telepathy over languages even though they have a full capability and a perfect opportunity to use both means of communications? First, they would need to rely on telepathy to communicate with all the living things for their soul farms. Second, they would have an issue with conflict or confusion if using both.

For instance, if we could utilize telepathy as well as languages to interact with others, wouldn't we have to deal with hugely serious problems unnecessarily on a daily basis? Especially when our souls or other people's souls would be immature to a certain degree for many respects, it would be quite easy for anyone to confuse or mislead others by either intention or mistake and cause terrible problems or tensions.

The result should be the same even if all the parties would be fully mature, for any souls should be imperfect to a perceivable degree no matter what and could make honest mistakes in communicating with others through both means. Given a choice, any smart beings should prefer telepathy to languages because it has no barriers unlike languages and it is superior to languages due to inherent comprehensiveness.

Hence, the supreme beings use telepathy rather than languages out of a matter of convenience through auxiliary means such as telepathic action, audio, dream, feeling, gaze, idea, image, imagination, insight, mail, phenomenon, smell, urge, thought, video, and so on so as to convey or exchange, i.e., send or receive, comprehensive messages. It is clearly more accurate, complete, efficient, fast, honest, and simple.

For a comparative discussion purpose with regard to two different means of communications, i.e., languages and telepathy, which should be better to let others know about a crime or accident scene right away that you do witness now? Regardless of linguistic ability, if you use a language, your message would contain all sorts of subjective discrepancies. Moreover, it would pose a language barrier to some people.

On the other hand, only if you should be capable of, what about using telepathy to do the same? Your telepathic message should consist of an exact imagery like a photo or a video clip which should be extremely objective as well as more accurate, complete, efficient, fast, honest, and simple. As illustrated, there exists no comparison whatsoever since comprehensive telepathy is inherently superior to languages.

Now, one late February morning in 2014, I went out to the side yard through the front door of our house as usual to pick up several newspapers tossed over the wooden gate. According to my decades-old habit, I should've come back directly afterwards and made coffee in the kitchen. I didn't. Instead, I found myself walking clear of the front door as if I were being pulled by someone all the way to the backyard.

With three newspapers tucked under my left armpit, I made a left turn and walked straight towards the backyard fence much like a sleepwalker or a zombie. To my surprise, I was totally out of my morning routine. I was thinking fast, but I couldn't figure out why I was even heading over there. Finally, I stopped at a spot for some reason and turned right. I happened to stand directly in front of the dragon plum tree.

The tree was about 15 feet tall. Thousands of pretty white flowers fully blossomed were mostly gone by then to be taken over by lots of baby green leaves ready to prosper. I could see all the branches since the leaves were still small. Soon I observed that there was something definitely wrong with a thin two-foot branch. It was protruding horizontally toward me. My nose was less than a foot away from its tip.

To my instinctive surprise, the whole branch surface was sprinkled with hundreds of tiny eggs ready to pop open. Luckily, no other branches appeared infested with the same. I felt somewhat relieved, but started panicking a little since I had no ideas initially on how to get rid of them. I became fearful that hundreds of harmful insects should be crawling out from them any moment so as to spread all over the tree.

After a brief session of brainstorming on what to do, I arranged to put a plastic bag over the branch and cut it off with a handsaw in order not to drop any eggs to the ground in the process. It took a while for me to finish the task, but it was a success. I felt incredible upon saving the plum tree. Ostensibly, it looked like a natural case of coincidence that I happened to walk over there, saw a problem, and solved it.

However, according to my subjective analysis of the rather shocking incident involving me, the deeply-troubled dragon plum tree mobilized me for a timely help. Why me? About four months earlier, it should have seen me help out the dwarf orange tree which was about 10 feet away from it. It had menacing white fungus spreading. Upon discovering, I patiently picked all of the contaminated leaves to rescue it.

Based on its observation memory over my action to save its neighbor tree, it should have decided to send me an SOS, expecting a positive response. How so? By telepathy? The questions instilled me a profound realization. Till then, a word of telepathy had not been on the front burner for me. Later on the same day, I in turn realized for sure that it was a telepathic mail which got me enlightened on July 7, 2006.

At the time, I did not know anything about telepathy per se, let alone all the mechanics of it. Accordingly, there were two errors in my subjective analysis delineated above. First, the dragon plum tree couldn't have processed a rather sophisticated chain of thought to obtain help, lacking a soul. Second, I as a human being couldn't have received a tree's telepathy directly since it was not from the supreme beings.

Only after understanding the mechanics of telepathy, I recognized that this is what must have happened in reality. Upon facing an urgent need to solve a problem, the dragon plum tree in our backyard sent a quick SOS telepathy to the supreme beings, for it could do so due to possessing a spirit while being alive. Based upon a review of goal congruence, the supreme beings moved to save the tree in their own way.

Upon realizing that I was a suitable candidate to do the job especially because of my prior experience in saving the dwarf orange tree in the same place, the supreme beings released the pause button installed already on the telepathic line between me and them and sent me an urgent telepathic action order to walk all the way to the troubled area so that I could rescue the dragon plum tree. It was awesome, wow!

Come to think of it, there should have been another reason why the supreme beings considered me as a suitable candidate to pull the job for the dragon plum tree in danger. Only days earlier on Sunday, February 23, 2014, there was another very strange event at our household. It was a sunny afternoon. We left the front door open to get some fresh air. For some reason, a black hummingbird flew into the house.

At first, it was quite entertaining to see the beautiful bird flying or hovering all over the dining and living rooms. The bird had a slender bill and fragile wings rapidly beating in order to stay exquisitely in the air. Of course, we opened all the sliding doors and windows as well immediately after, but the bird would not go back out over three or four hours. Rather than sitting, the bird would constantly float in the air.

We employed all sorts of methods to let the bird out, but to no avail. Whirling a broomstick around did not work. A dangled glass bowl filled with honey water was of no use. Over the time, we could see the bird become gradually frail and weak presumably due to frustration over not being able to sip cool nutritious nectar from pungent flowers outdoors. Soon, we got genuinely concerned on the bird's well-being.

After all, we ended up creating a makeshift bird trap with a coat hanger, a big piece of cloth, and our broomstick. It was a cinch for me to snatch the bird with it. With a sigh of relief, we freed the black hummingbird into the blue sky. After being released, the bird frantically flew up into the air, stopped a little high up, turned around to face us looking up, hovered a bit as if bowing, and sped away. It was awesome.

What was a point of telling you this additional story? The supreme beings should have observed from their planet our whole rescuing event from start to finish. Even though most of the actual event took place inside our house, it was entirely possible for them to see since at least a beam or ray of light from them could easily come in through open doors or windows and bounce or reflect everywhere in the rooms.

With regard to a light penetration, it should never be a prerequisite for telepathy in general used by all the spirits except for the human spirits. Since we have a spirit as well as a soul, we do have a telepathic capability as well, but our receiving function is paused, being different from our intact sending function. As a result, a constant two-way feedback through telepathy is out of reach, requiring a visual contact.

Incidentally, as demonstrated so clearly through the light penetration test conducted by those four zombies sent by the association in the Scene 4 of my telepathic Dream A previously analyzed, the light penetration feature would be extremely important in telepathic communications between the human beings and the supreme beings. One by one, the supreme beings taught me all of the mechanics of telepathy.

ELEVEN:
Mechanics of Telepathy (2)

In the course of writing this extremely strange book, I had to pick up almost all about the mechanics of telepathy. Once it became obvious to me that the supreme beings were to clearly teach me all about it in every which way possible, I kind of started experimenting on my own with all my tools in order to confirm this or that for thorough understanding. No matter what I experienced and learned so far, of course, all the mechanics of telepathy could or would not be proven scientifically simply because critical aspects are controlled not by the human beings but by the supreme beings for real.

As a matter of real life, homeless people and nudists could survive well without homes and clothes, respectively. Even so, the human beings would require food, shelter, and clothing for survival. Food is most essential. Without food, we die. Among all the living things, only we would require shelter and clothing as well. We must be very insecure and vulnerable. For real, our bodies require them, not our souls.

If so, our female and male souls are suitable for any space travel and extreme planetary living environments just like all the unisex bodies of the supreme beings. Yeah, that is right. To our surprise, the supreme beings do not require food, shelter, and clothing for survival. Further, they don't even breathe air or drink water to live. In fact, their unisex bodies never grow old to die eventually once manufactured.

Also, their fully mature female and male souls taken or harvested from their own soul farms around the universe never grow old to die later, either. Then, can you see what is really going on? This is how or why the supreme beings can truly enjoy living an eternal life in countless corners of the vast universe. They never die. They never worry about earning a living to secure food, shelter, and clothing, either.

As such, they could reside literally almost anywhere in the boundless wide-open universe. Given all these, a lot of them should freely relocate to any other planets, thereby having a constant pragmatic need to multiply by themselves. They could manufacture as many brand-new souls just like bodies to utilize, but getting the souls fully mature could be toughest unless all the living things on soul farms cooperate.

For this practical reason, the supreme beings have a constant need to communicate through telepathy with most living things including at least some human beings so as to achieve their harvest needs and targets of fully mature souls as efficiently as possible. As for me, they do have a serious stake in teaching me everything about the whole mechanics of telepathy to convey me the whole big picture as intended.

Equipped with a rather wholesome understanding of what it really is and how it actually works, I began to notice that an awful lot of baffling, enigmatic, mysterious, strange, unexplainable, unnatural or weird events or things could be logically explained and understood if we put our mind to it. At this point of discussions over the mechanics of telepathy, I would like to take on actual happenings and analyze them.

First, with few exceptions, the human beings dream while sleeping day or night. There are two types of dreams, typical and nontypical. The former depicts all those regular dreams that we dream and forget almost at once. The latter depicts all those rare unusual dreams which we could never forget about a factual content for a long time even for years. They should be telepathic dreams from the supreme beings.

Most of the unforgettable nontypical dreams would be precognitive in nature by providing a foreknowledge on anything good or bad, which might happen later in real life. For this segment of our discussion, I would like to focus on some of those strange but real dreams related to pregnancy. They have been widely known as conception dreams in the Far East region for thousands of years per historical records.

However, those dreams tend to occur not prior to or right at the moment of conception, but sometime afterwards during pregnancy before childbirth for sure. According to a great deal of such real-life dreams recalled by lots of people not only in the Far East areas but also probably everywhere, only pregnant mothers and people close to them experience. I would call them humanization dreams instead to be exact.

What? Based on what I have learned so far in terms of the mechanics of telepathy as well as the earth soul farm operations by the supreme beings, the answer is pretty clear. Soon after insertion of either a brand-new or a reincarnated soul into a fetus with his or her brain sufficiently developed, the supreme beings instill or send a unique telepathic dream symbolizing a child's future into a pregnant mother's brain.

Meantime, if the supreme beings could not carry out the above as a final humanization action right away for any reason whatsoever, they might instead send such a precious humanization dream most likely to mother of the expectant mother or father of the fetus immediately or sometime later. Hopefully, it would make a complete sense to those people who experienced such a telepathic dream without realizing.

Second, when I began working on this extraordinary book on November 6, 2014, I started to recognize through a gradual awareness that something fascinating was going on with my serious lingering neck pain which I had developed by falling asleep mistakenly in a wrong position on a couch while sitting down by myself to watch TV on May 26, 2014. I still had a constant pain at the time after over five months.

In order to fix my problem, thankfully, four medical professionals, i.e., my primary physician, physical therapist, chiropractor, and therapeutic masseuse, tried to help me out with their best during the agonizing months to no avail. At one point after an adjustment session, my chiropractor even suggested me to start learning how to use my left hand for a mouse in front of my computer in order to alleviate the pain.

At first, I never realized what was going on with me. Soon, I gradually started noticing that I was not feeling any neck pain whenever I was working on the book at my desk. However, whenever I was working on something else at my desk with the same exact computer, mouse, and so on in the same exact sitting position, I always suffered from the pain. On a pain scale, the former vs. the latter equaled to 0 vs. 10.

No matter how many times I would experiment with myself in my office, I would witness the same exact results. It was absolutely baffling since it was obviously real to me. After one week or so, I had to acknowledge on my own that the supreme beings were actually gazing at the same screen over my shoulder and clearly helping me to keep on writing. It was a telepathic phenomenon that lasted for three months.

Third, speaking of my computer, I've been working with a nice Apple MacBook Pro. It has never failed me for years of service except for only once on February 25, 2015. It was 3:30 a.m. I just began to think about calling it a day. Suddenly, my laptop quit itself completely although I never shut it down or turned it off myself. I was totally confused and shaken off over what had just happened to my machine.

Out of curiosity, I ended up rebooting my computer and scanning for virus right then and there. I did not know why it had happened because no computer virus was found. Only then, it dawned on me clearly that the supreme beings should have agreed with my thought and acted out to make me fully aware of such a point by outlandishly turning it off. Even if things occur behind your back, you could figure out.

In fact, I was just reviewing my work after finishing a telepathy portion related to the subject of soul vs. spirit in Chapter 9. I then sensed that the whole subject of telepathy contained far more than I could handle within the particular segment and that I should call it a day and go home to sleep. For real, the supreme beings showed me a telepathic action. By the way, they operate UFOs similarly through telepathy.

Fourth, about the obnoxious stench that I smelled in the middle room of our house from February 12 through 15 in 2015, which was taken up to corroborate facts on soul vs. spirit in Chapter 8, I figured out how it must have happened. Later on February 23, 2015, after midnight, I switched over to the middle room to spend that night since one of our kids returned home from Los Angeles for a personal trip to Italy.

Unexpectedly, I detected a modest trace of the same foul odor. It quickly turned unbearably terrible by 1:00 a.m. I naturally looked around to find out what was contributing to a sudden intensity of the smell. The only thing I noticed was a directional opening of the horizontal Venetian blinds that was blocking a view from the sky, thereby denying any light getting down from the night sky. Hence, I corrected it.

As I expected with an absolute degree of confidence, there was no such obnoxious odor whatsoever found in the whole middle room when I opened my eyes in the morning. Apparently, I was able to convince the supreme beings that they could still send me their telepathic messages without a hitch because I corrected a directional opening of the blinds. Obviously, they exercised a technique for a telepathic odor.

Most likely, there was a dead mouse in a crawlspace of the middle room ceiling, which might have consumed rat poison anywhere around the neighborhood and rested there. The supreme beings must have coordinated an activity level of single-celled decomposing bacteria on the dead body by sending out timely telepathic action orders. All the monads possess spirits that do not require a light penetration feature.

Fifth, in the middle of January 2015, I got very sick from a rather fascinating flu virus for seven days. Actually, I was even bedridden for three days. From its start to finish, I felt so weak in general. Throughout the whole sequential process of sickness, I experienced or kind of tasted in a way virtually all of possible flu symptoms. I had never had such a horrendous yet unbelievably comprehensive flu in my life.

To my astonishment, I had to suffer from exactly 24 different agonizing symptoms such as queasy stomach, skin poking, sneeze, extreme fever, runny nose, backache, body chill, itchy throat, eyeball pain, urine reduction, body swell, kidney slowdown, fatigue, watery eyes, diarrhea, body ache, anal heat, exhaustion, drowsiness, gas release, appetite loss, dizziness, cough, and headache. It ended with sticky sweat.

From its onset, I felt a desolate, illogical, and strong telepathic urge from the supreme beings not to take any pill. I decided to fight the flu virus head-on that I had contracted accidentally around a heavily-coughing lady in a drugstore aisle a day earlier. Thus I did not even take a single aspirin. It was like riding on a dangerous yet exciting roller coaster. In hindsight, it was a natural body flush, purifying my soul.

Sixth, after spending time in big oceans, how could salmons journey thousands of miles to their respective natal rivers? Do they have a GPS navigator? No, absolutely not. Scientific theories suggest that they might use geomagnetic and chemical imprinting. Yet, they have no soul to achieve such sophistication. In reality, the supreme beings send out timely telepathic action orders to govern salmon migrations.

Seventh, have you seen a flock of birds in flight or a school of fish in swim? Amazing, isn't it? What is a secret? Since they all possess a spirit and a pair of eyes, they utilize a telepathic gaze by themselves to maintain their formation. Speaking of eyes, virtually all animals and insects have two for a depth perception or telepathic gaze. All pets like dogs use them to sense our love as well. Love holds no language.

Eighth, if the living things perish, their spirits expire, too. Unlike our souls, they could never escape dead bodies. Naturally they are so obedient and suitable for support roles. No matter how bizarre any telepathic action orders from the supreme beings are, they obey. My aunt witnessed one day that a huge tiger showed up out of nowhere for a guard duty at her overnight prayers behind a Buddhist temple in Seoul.

TWELVE:

Anatomy of Our Prayers (1)

While a linguistic communication means is for souls, a telepathic communication means is for spirits. Factually, the former is built on languages while the latter isn't. As a result, the former has linguistic components while the latter does not. Now, here comes a slight complication. Because we have a spirit, we could send a telepathic message, but it should mostly contain linguistic components built in a soul. Then, any receiving parties should be able to decipher it by way of a linguistic soul action alike. Thus only the supreme beings could receive and process such a telepathic message.

At four o'clock in the afternoon of January 20, 2015, I dropped by a neighborhood convenience store to check up on my lottery tickets. As I passed by a gentleman sitting up against a pillar close to the entrance, he told me in a barely audible voice that he was homeless. I stood in line to claim a tiny winning, but for some reason I was captivated by his genuinely polite demeanor. I made up my mind to see him.

Giving one third of my prize money, I told him that it was my lottery winning. Into my totally unprepared soul, he told me that he would pray for me and that he was going to church every Sunday. He pointed his finger to a parking lot when I accidentally asked him where he lived. I was so sorry. He added that he was attending a community church and repeated that he would pray for me. I thanked him fitly.

He was a very short person with a dark complexion, wearing a brownish jacket and black pants. He looked like a Latino with fluent English. His hands were clean and soft. As our abrupt small talk ended, I briskly turned to the right to walk to my car only several steps away. I got shocked to see that he vanished completely in split seconds. Although I kept looking around for him, he was nowhere to be found.

Pulling out of there, I prayed for him to the supreme beings in my car. I felt a sudden increase in moisture level of my eyes. In fact, no one is immune from being homeless if something goes terribly wrong. I realized in the evening that I had dreamt a telepathic dream in the wee hours of the very day, in which I had seen a black shoe at the exact spot of the shopping strip where I happened to run into him later.

In the above odd episode, he would apparently pray to God, but I prayed to the supreme beings in charge of me. Everyone would understand his prayer, but virtually no one would understand my prayer at least for a while if disclosed. Although I have been exposed to a fair number of different religions in my life, I have never taken in any particular one. 'NO PREF' was impressed even on my U.S. Army dog tags.

Even so, I am like a gnostic theist since I am neither agnostic nor atheistic. Yet, I do not believe in any religious God or gods created by the human beings purely in our soul. They are all neither visible nor part of the physical universe. Instead of those, I do believe a generic god installed by the supreme beings, which exists in our soul as a perfect being. For my sanity, I don't pray to gods whether religious or not.

Soon after I started to work on this fascinating book, I have begun to pray for the first time in my life. However, it is to the supreme beings overseeing my soul or this book project. In the meantime, I do not doubt eyewitness reports claiming actual encounters with the supreme beings all over the globe. Certainly, they are so visible and must be part of the physical universe per my understanding of them as well.

All of the prayers made by the human beings would reach the supreme beings, i.e., the respective soul managers, caring for all the respective individual prayers regardless of any or no religions. A prayer is really a telepathic message. A praying is nothing but submitting a telepathic message to a soul manager of a praying person. No exceptions, period. Religious gods are perfect but fictional thus playing no part.

Unlike a soul, a spirit has no sophisticated cognitive thinking ability, thus unable to accommodate religious gods. By this logic, such gods could play no part in any telepathic communications and in turn no part in any religious prayers, except in virtually all the religious activities fundamentally and grossly misled. A misunderstanding of facts on soul vs. spirit has culminated in the current human mess in religions.

Just by lurking around in our soul whether religious or not, all those fictional thus perfect religious gods seem to serve no practical purpose except to give birth to delusional or mistaken belief and resultant doubtful or fragile comfort. Nevertheless, the supreme beings have been warm and wise enough to leave all the religious gods alone so long as they would contribute to improving maturity of any human souls.

Are there any religions on the earth, which do away with prayers? No, apparently not. Could any nonreligious person pray, too? Yes, of course. Look at me for example. Whether religious or not, all the human beings on the earth could pray anyhow anytime anywhere if they wish to do so. Since we possess a spirit while being alive, we could send a telepathic message to the supreme beings over such a spirit.

In other words, our human prayers would be always received by only the supreme beings no matter which form of religious gods we might worship or not. In a nutshell, all our prayers would have nothing to do with any religions per se since they are purely a telepathic message to the supreme beings for receiving and for further processing with a result if and only if each prayer wish meets a goal congruence test.

Now, I would like to cut open our prayers to expose their factual anatomy by way of an extraordinary individual whom I used to know for nearly 12 years while growing up. Why him? A day after I asked the supreme beings to assist me for this chapter, they responded and sent me a short but clever thus smart telepathic dream between 10:00 p.m. and midnight on May 1, 2015, in which he appeared at our door.

For decades, I used to go to bed well after midnight. It was quite different on that Friday night. As soon as I did finish watching a nice warm romantic comedy movie titled 'Heaven Is Waiting' on Netflix close to 10:00 p.m., I felt so drowsy that I could not stay up or around. In the middle of my two-hour nap, I received a super-brief telepathic dream from the supreme beings. Wow, I could not forget about it.

According to a clear and concise voice in my dream, I was to open up the door so as to meet someone important even though there was no ringing of a doorbell that I heard. I opened the door of our very house. It was so dark outside. To my complete surprise, standing in front of the door was Heavenly Mercy Grandpa. It was his only Korean name in translation that was known to us including me and my aunt.

I said wow, greeted him by his name, and asked him whether he could still recognize me after all the years apart. Of course, he knew who I was, but he could not talk readily due to being frozen promptly out of a mesmerizing surprise. He looked exactly the same as before in his 70s to exhibit a dark wrinkled complexion with baldness on top of his head. Even his dirty, old, and thick clothes looked familiar to me.

As I recall vividly, he used to wear exactly the same grey-colored raggedy monk clothes no matter how cold and freezing in the winter or how hot and humid in the summer. He did not appear to wash his clothes at all perhaps because he had no extra pair of the monk clothes to wear in between. Further, he didn't appear to have bathed or washed his face or hands for months. He looked homeless, but had no odor.

He was a self-ordained Buddhist monk. He resided alone in a tiny Buddhist temple that he mostly built himself on the side of the big Generous King Mountain overlooking downtown Seoul right after the bloody Korean War stopped in 1953. Even though he had a modest number of followers, he used to visit their homes individually because his temple was too small to accommodate all for any religious services.

According to my up-close observations from time to time over a decade or so, he was very good at telling about past or future happenings on his followers in his own terms. He didn't seem intelligent or sharp, but he was honest, kind, and very mature in taking care of other people. I never saw him ask for money in exchange for all the fortune-telling or religious services. Certainly, he was not in it for the money.

As a result, he was dirt poor just like us scraping by. With an advanced level of foretelling capability on matters related to life in general, he could or should have made lots of money if he wanted to, but he chose not to. He regularly performed all sorts of religious services for us at his temple. Although we could only appreciate for his work by sharing a meal once in a while, he never treated us as less important.

Based upon his sincere explanations to us, he was in constant consultations with various Buddhist saints up there. Apparently, as a simple-minded boy growing up, I couldn't believe almost anything out of his mouth because the whole thing did not make any sense to me, but I never doubted his sincerity as a decent, honest, mature, and sane human being. With all my heart, I respected him, but kept a watchful eye.

I was able to observe him carefully numerous times when he appeared to communicate with his Buddhist saints. It seemed to happen any moment anywhere. Even during a normal conversation with my aunt while sharing a meal, he often got in touch with them to obtain timely answers to my aunt's questions. His posture was never an issue with them for sure even if he sat down freely with his eyes wide-open.

At this point, I should talk about a real-life incident which I witnessed the whole event taking place at our home in 1966 or 1967. My aunt had two daughters and two sons. They were all grown-ups who lived apart, but she managed to take her elder son in to care for because he suffered from an illness unknown. He saw quite a few doctors to no avail. After being bedridden for months, he looked like a skeleton.

One day, our Heavenly Mercy Grandpa visited us at home. Even before he set his foot in the door, he knew that there was someone seriously sick in our scanty rented room. Within minutes, he was consulting with his Buddhist saints while sitting down on the bare floor next to the sick patient. Upon getting an image, i.e., a telepathic image, he asked us to remove from our kitchen a piece of wood partially burnt.

After he left, lo and behold, we actually found such a thing underneath a freestanding cupboard against the wall. When we moved in, we must have put it there to stabilize it. Her elder son started to get better immediately after getting rid of it and recovered fully in a couple of weeks. In fact, it was absolutely a real-life miracle to us, which I did witness. Apparently, they must've sent him to us for a timely rescue.

Who were they in fact? They were not his Buddhist saints as our Heavenly Mercy Grandpa truly believed at the time due to his lack of knowledge on the whole big picture. They were the supreme beings. Obviously, he did not even know that his communication means was a simple telepathy. Further, he definitely didn't even realize that all his prayers or questions to them were nothing but a telepathic message.

As demonstrated herein, each and every human soul on the earth, i.e., a soul farm, is managed by one or more of the supreme beings designated with such an incredible task. An individual supreme being may handle quite a multitude of souls from insertion to separation, i.e., from life to death of each body as well as throughout numerous reincarnation cycles as planned for a full maturity of each and every soul.

By this practical reason, no matter how good or bad a current life cycle is, each and every human soul would be extremely precious to the supreme beings in charge of such a soul. As a result, they would not hesitate in assigning any so-called guardian angels to assure a well-being of any soul if and only if a situation demands. Further, they would not hesitate in listening to our prayers carefully with an interest.

THIRTEEN:

Anatomy of Our Prayers (2)

The supreme beings are utterly pragmatic by nature. They would love to apply a doctrine of substance over form whenever and wherever just like any mature human beings. To them, any ornamental bells and whistles would be of no use unless they serve a practical purpose. In this rationale, they did not make such embellishments a prerequisite when they installed a telepathic function in a corner of our spirit. Hence, the human beings could pray, i.e., send a telepathic message to the supreme beings, in a light-penetrable space without any formats, limitations or restrictions whatsoever.

With regard to a light-penetrable space, why would it be necessary solely for the human beings to communicate with the supreme beings? Originally, they designed us that way to satisfy a practical need for visual feedback on all the human beings sending a telepathic message, i.e., offering a prayer, to identify its sender and validate a situation prior to releasing a pause button if warranted for an answer or reply.

According to a streamlined design of our spirit with respect to a telepathic function, human prayers or telepathic messages from a light-blocked area would not even be sent, let alone reaching the supreme beings. Meanwhile, a beam of light mostly travels straight in the universe including the earth atmosphere unless it gets totally absorbed or partially reflected upon engaging a liquid or solid object obstructing.

Even if a modest amount of light goes into a closed space through a crack or opening, it bounces off here, there, and everywhere on all the interior surface areas infinitely if it is strong enough, thereby illuminating the whole space so that any objects in the space could be visible. As illustrated, light can penetrate darkness, thus at night as well. As such, it is absolutely possible for them to observe us day or night.

What degree of natural light penetrability in a space should be adequate enough to accommodate human prayers? Without turning on any of the lighting equipment or fixture, if you can see your face in a mirror comfortably during the day, it should be good enough. As long as you're in such a space, your prayers would be transmitted to them without a hitch day or night whether any electrical lights are on or off.

In addition, it should be a very good idea for you to accommodate a light penetration angle by adjusting interior decoration materials whenever needed and workable so that they could see you clearly from up there on their planets in the universe.   I confirmed this critical aspect of a telepathic communications with the supreme beings based on my own experiment with horizontal Venetian blinds and bad stench.

In fact, if x can see y, y can see x, too, given there is no view blocker. From their planet up there in the universe, a beam of light would travel straight into a window of your praying space. On its way, it would rarely have an event of bouncing off and changing a direction of travel. As a result, securing a solid light penetration angle is a prerequisite for telepathic exchanges with the supreme beings handling you.

What is an interconnection between a beam of light and visual feedback? I would introduce a hypothetical case. If you could spot a person walking with a flashlight at night, the person could see only up to where a beam of light from the flashlight ends to illuminate. If the light gets obstructed by an object, the person could see virtually nothing beyond. To sum up, replace the flashlight with a night vision device.

In fact, all the supreme beings possess a night vision. Moreover, their beam of light bouncing off everywhere in a confined space seems to carry an ultimate camera. As such, they can hear or see us 24/7. Besides, they don't even sleep. Then, how could they identify each of us from all the others? By DNAs, fingerprints or pupils? Well, those methods are for a randomly-produced body that decomposes after death.

Please keep in mind that any human body is nothing but a temporary container for an eternal soul which may go through a number of life cycles using a different body each time until it gets matured fully while on the earth soul farm and carried by the supreme beings to a distant planet for an eternal life. As such, they have a practical need to identify each of us by our soul and use invisible soul prints to do so.

Now, based upon what we have discussed so far on the anatomy of our prayers, I would entertain you with four actual examples of our prayers to further the understanding. First, let's revisit the place where a huge tiger showed up in the middle of night and stayed up next to my aunt till dawn. She was there at the sacred spot behind the small temple all by herself with her candles lit to pray to all Buddhist saints.

The temple was a place of Buddhist rituals built and maintained by our Heavenly Mercy Grandpa, which was on Generous King Mountain in Seoul. Down below, the busy downtown was visible, accommodating several old palaces as well as the Blue House functioning like the White House in the United States. For security reason, he asked my aunt to stay at the temple during his out-of-town overnight travel.

Instead of sleeping at night, she decided to dedicate her own solitary prayers to all Buddhist saints all night long. After having a quick dinner at the temple, she went over to the sacred spot with a bowl of spring water and a handful of candlesticks. Quietly, she started to pray. She kept praying. Clearly, there was no one else in the vicinity after sundown. According to what she told me later, she felt a little nervous.

It was at midnight. All of a sudden, out of nowhere, the huge tiger showed up slowly and sat down right next to her. To her amazement, instead of being scared in any way, she became comfortable and undisturbed all throughout her overnight prayers. She acknowledged that the tiger seemed determined to be quite alert during her entire praying hours. Near dawn, the tiger got up and disappeared out of her sight.

When she mentioned her unbelievable experience to Heavenly Mercy Grandpa, he could never comprehend any encounter with such a tiger although he actually lived there. As she came back home, she described it to me vividly, too. According to my memory, it was certainly in the mid-1960s. Was there a tiger in that era in the middle of crowded Seoul? It was unheard of at the time, but I never doubted her story.

Fortunately, I'm currently in an astonishing position to analyze the esoteric situation so that it could make sense. Lacking knowledge on telepathy, Heavenly Mercy Grandpa probably did not recognize an importance of a natural light penetrability when he made his own Buddhist temple there. According to my memory saved from a couple of visits, the whole temple had only one small building with no windows.

A golden statue of Buddha worshiped was too huge for the size of the temple. Most likely, the dark temple was built around and over. Surely, it was not suited for prayers. Perhaps that is precisely why he had to search and set up an outdoor sacred spot right behind the temple so that he could readily contact Buddhist saints, i.e., the supreme beings for real, or vice versa in order to deal with so many life puzzles.

Rationally speaking, my aunt could and did transmit a barrage of full telepathic messages to the supreme beings in charge of her soul in the prayer session at the sacred spot. As the night deepened, they got concerned about her safety and sent a timely telepathic action order to a guardian angel, i.e., a roving tiger, to keep her from any harm all night long. Any living thing with a spirit can serve as a guardian angel.

Resting upon a grossly-misguided religious belief or faith derived from inaccurate or incomplete teaching which lacked inopportunely the most pressing factual information on the whole big picture of universal life system operations, she only thought that she was praying to Buddhist saints or Buddha himself who had gotten awakened or enlightened at age 35 and taught Buddhism for 45 years till death in India.

His earthly name was Siddhartha Gautama. Clearly, he was a real human being with a spirit in addition to a soul. As he passed away before 400 B.C.E., his fully mature soul departed his body and it was most definitely escorted by the supreme beings to their eternal world elsewhere. However, his bodily spirit had to remain with his dead body to perish in accordance with the universal life system operation rules.

No matter how holy his spirit seemed to believers as he taught his religion devised from a sudden enlightenment felt through a telepathic mail during his prayers under a tree, such a holy spirit was also nothing but a usual bodily spirit and thus it was surely ended or perished with his dead body. For real, his holy or bodily spirit seemed alive while he was, but it became deceased or nonexistent after his bodily death.

Second, earthly prayers are nothing but a telepathic message that should come from a piece of thought in a soul. Sometimes such thought would be sent automatically to the supreme beings, or they could read our mind by themselves. For this, I would talk about my own fascinating experience. English is not my native language since I was not born here. When I came here in 1975, I was exactly like a deaf person.

Despite taking English for 7 years at school, I could not hear or speak a word of it upon arrival in San Francisco via Honolulu, for I had no chance of learning its real sound. I still cherish those who stimulated me linguistically. Fresh off the plane, Ms. Soin struggled with me at an adult school. In a U.S. Army boot camp, Mr. Boaz pushed me really hard. Joseph Smith taught me all about the real sound of English.

The last person was one of the direct descendants of Joseph Smith who founded the Mormon Church. He was a bunk buddy during a basic combat training in Fort Leonard Wood, Missouri, in 1975. The supreme beings made him a guardian angel to assist me out of a psychological hardship caused by a severe language barrier so that I could become a productive member of society in a newly-adopted country.

In 2007, I found myself proficient enough to collect, edit, format, and translate English jokes to publish 'English Jokes' for Koreans so that a real sound of English could be picked up directly to hear to talk without a language barrier. While at it, I perfected a way to write down actual sound of English accurately in Korean with all 24 phonetic alphabets in plain Hangul invented by King Sejong the Great in 1446.

I scrutinized phonetic components of two languages. I isolated 9 pieces of English sound, which are absent from Korean sound. I could not properly record them in Korean. They formed the nasty English language barrier to Koreans. One night, I got a vivid telepathic dream that I never asked for, in which the King himself in his golden regalia showed me two ingenious but simple ways to solve the whole thing.

Third, as explained in detail before, my excruciating neck pain was off or on so clearly for 27 days depending on whether I worked on this book or not. Finally, I got fed up. On December 3, 2014, I calmly shouted at them in English not to play with me, demanded 'a permanent solution', and forgot all about it. One of my friends, serving in New York as a Presbyterian church elder, phoned me three hours later.

In the middle of our normal conversation in Korean, he abruptly asked me how I was doing with my own health. Casually, I told him about my neck pain. Quite shockingly, he told me in English that he had 'a permanent solution' for me. He insisted on teaching me how to exercise my painful neck while ignoring a pain. I did it religiously for 2 months. It worked. The supreme beings must have responded, wow!

Fourth, ever since, I've been completely free of pain except on April 29, 2015. I was cleaning a bathroom faucet. I picked a random YouTube clip on extraterrestrials on my iPhone. The same huge neck pain started. When it uttered a wrong view about us being their slaves, they turned it off. After I pledged to the supreme beings not to watch it again, the pain stopped at once, wow! I felt their factual presence.

FOURTEEN:
Factual Nature of Religion

Unlike the human or supreme beings, god is perfect. Such a perfect god would exist forever in our imperfect soul. Just like our soul, god is not visible in the physical universe because god is nothing but a fictional generic perfect being. It is purely a concept. So, god cannot die. God is not dead. Since we are so imperfect, we cannot afford to lose our god. As a matter of fact, we cannot afford to lose our religion in which such a perfect god should be loved on a factual basis. Virtually all earthly religions are going in wrong directions. The supreme beings are quite concerned about the situation.

What is religion? It is a road map for a human soul. It should indicate one and only destination for full maturity. However, there may be numerous different routes to follow no matter where each person may journey from on the earth. Each route represents a respective religion for its followers. Any human being could even establish his or her own route without using a suggested route paved by a certain religion.

Please keep in mind that you should always strive to near closer to the one and only destination for full maturity. If your route or religion would never take you there, get off and get onto another route or devise your own correct route. Your life is too precious and short to be wasted on the road. By now, you should recognize that it does not really matter which religion or route you follow so long as you get there.

Perfection has truly nothing to do with imperfection. If it does, it ought to be imperfect. No perfect beings create imperfect beings. We are imperfect. Our body is so fragile. Our soul induces ludicrous thoughts as well. Consequently, a perfect god didn't create our ancestors. Lacking differing transitional forms, we are not a product of evolution, either. The imperfect supreme beings or tacs created us on science.

As discussed earlier, the supreme beings possess the same soul as ours, being thus imperfect. Suitably, they are not gods but tacs. If then, would they believe in gods? No, but they do believe in a fictional generic perfect god which also exists in their imperfect soul. Howbeit, they believe in no religions, for they possess no need. Their soul is already fully mature. No matter what, they worry about ours. Why?

First, we still kill each other in the name of religions. When you usually create or make anything from scratch for real, there must be a very good reason. Likewise, when the supreme beings originally created the human beings as well as all the other living things situated on the earth soul farm, there must have been a very good reason for all the species. Apparently, all the living things are very important to them.

Animals hardly kill one another in the same species, not being cannibal. Neither do insects, monads, and plants. What is wrong with the human beings? All over the places, we kill fellow beings all the time in conflict, crime, war, etc. To the eyes of the supreme beings, it is actually nothing but a pure waste no matter what a reason may be. How about a religious killing? Of course, it is even absurd to most of us.

If you commit, i.e., lead or participate in, a religious killing of any kind, what do you practically gain? Nothing. Such a senseless killing would bring about more killings in retaliation and tragic back-and-forth killings could continue. The supreme beings view all religious killings as extremely immature. Such killings defeat the very purpose of religion and hurt their soul farm output to a point of total frustration.

Unfortunately, human history is full of such killings. Even today, terrorists kill innocent people for bogus beliefs planted or fake rewards promised by false religious dogmas. Going forward, as the earthly human beings get enlightened on the whole big picture, most people would finally realize a factual goal of life and willingly adopt a corrective action. The human beings shall cooperate with the supreme beings.

Second, a god shall never be born as a human being, for the former is purely a fictional perfect being invisible in the physical universe while the latter is an actual imperfect being visible in the physical universe. They are two totally different beings much like, for example, apples and oranges. Similarly, a human being could not be born as a god, either. Have you noticed an invisible human being or a visible god?

To put it bluntly, the supreme beings do not want us to make god out of human or human out of god. In fact, no humans produce apple out of orange or orange out of apple. If anyone claims as such, it is purely a deception or sorcery. If any religions claim such a thing, they should be dogmatic, coercing their followers for an absolute belief, faith or trust. If your dress shirt were buttoned up wrong, you'd correct it.

There is a simple reason why a human being cannot be or become a god although a perfect god already exists in a corner of his or her own soul no matter what. Because we have hands long enough to reach or touch our own genitalia, no human female or male could stay away from any sexual temptation. For real, our upper body with a godlike brain is firmly adjoined to our lower body with animalistic genitalia.

In fact, all the earthly religions were founded by the human beings since they all had body parts including brain and genitalia. Then, no religions were founded by any gods or their relatives for that matter. Realistically, revealing the fact against the myth may not be easy, but there is no other way. Instead of holding onto your truth that is totally false, embrace the fact that everybody on the earth would believe.

Third, no particular religion could be entitled to any exclusive claims or rights to all the human beings and their surroundings in the universe. Well, that is a common sense, but our religious atmosphere appears to ignore such a point. Consequently, even though a countless number of religious dogmas across the board on the earth have been formulated for such a narrow selfish view, none does anything about it.

Historically speaking, most religions as well as their reckless or thoughtless followers have committed numerous heinous acts against humanity based upon such a misguided dogmatic belief. Even today, countless immature conducts originated from religious hatred or superiority must be very rampant in most parts of the earth. In the whole big picture, on the road map for full maturity, all the religions are equal.

In this respect, some of the mature religious leaders tend to display a sign of hope because they seem to be quite open to coexistence with other religions under no prejudice. However, many others who hold onto an obsolete or wrong road map showing only their lousy route to full maturity for not only their followers but also all the other human beings still exhibit a sign of hopelessness. They need to be reborn.

Such a disparity among competing religions as well as their respective mindless followers including leaders and supporters germinates from a limited knowledge basis since the whole big picture on the universal life system operation has never been frankly exposed to the earthly human beings. In the past, a complete set of the whole big picture was not even given to any religious founders by the supreme beings.

Fourth, as a natural consequence of utilizing only an incomplete set available at the most if any, all the religious founders and their dedicated close helpers had to work with partial information which had lots of holes in it everywhere. In order to fill those holes in the process, they relied on one of our peculiar human soul characteristics, i.e., dreaming up a story whether feasible or not, thus creating a lot of myths.

In fact, all dogmatic scriptures written for respective earthly religions have been rather full of mystical elements. In other words, they should be most likely a combination of fact and fiction, i.e., faction. Either by chance or by design, most religious scriptures were developed in a way that most readers should really have a difficult time in distinguishing between factual and fictional elements. That is not honesty.

Whoever asks legitimate questions about a mystical portion of the scriptures would not get any straight answers. In any religions, there is a sophisticated system of coercion pressing for absolute belief, faith or trust from the followers. As a result, if you could not tolerate their illogical coercion, you would decide not to follow their route on the road map. Indeed, virtually all modern religions keep losing followers.

Could it be possible for the human beings to follow a religion that would be built on factual information only so that all ordinary people on the road would never even have any head-scratching questions on the religion and scriptures? Yes, of course, there will be a day for such a new beginning. Sane people would flock to a religion designed or realigned logically, for it would provide a factual sense. Let's watch.

Fifth, unfortunately, most earthly religions scarcely exercise pragmatism with a doctrine of substance over form. As stressed before, even the supreme beings firmly exercise pragmatism in their eternal life in order not to waste limited resources and damage natural environments in the universe. They don't breathe, drink, eat or wear. They don't produce garbage or waste. They draw circles or signs only on crops.

Just look around where you are located on the earth. Do you see any religions without such bells and whistles as decorative facilities, elaborate instruments and statues, and showy uniforms for religious service providers as well as a complex series of ceremonies? No, perhaps not. You may even find some religions with very lavish religious facilities built with excessive donations from the burdened followers.

What would they have to do with making your soul more mature under religions? Nothing. As a matter of fact, all those superficial bells and whistles are not a prerequisite for a religion per se. Apparently, except for demonstrating their bureaucratic religious authority to their own followers, they provide no practical value for promoting inner growth. The supreme beings want people to resort to the very basics.

A business exists for money, but a religion does not. The business deals with goods and services, but the religion our souls. Religious services shall never be sold for money. Hence, the religion does not and should not exist for money. On the contrary, certain religions appear to be managed like a business for money, thereby paying their most attention to form rather than substance. It is time for a new philosophy.

Sixth, as precisely defined at the start of this chapter, religion is just a road map for a human soul whose job here on the earth is to strive to be fully mature in life if possible. To believers, a respective religion serves as a safe and short route to full maturity only if their route proves to be correct. As such, religious textbook materials play a significant role. Modernize them since there are a lot of changes to be made.

Otherwise, they would fall behind others or become irrelevant to be obsolete. Instead of working under dubious unpersuasive dogmatic coercion strategies over any and all illogical or mystical elements, call upon clarity and honesty. It is another myth on its own that religious materials should carry mystical elements. It should be fairly simple to apply the whole big picture. All the clouds shall disappear easily.

Incidentally, you might not be able to find a suitable religion for full maturity because there should be too many options or your cherished soul should be uniquely different. If so, stop looking for it and get out of your way to observe the whole road map from above. As mentioned before, you could even develop your own correct route on the road map. Since you also have a perfect god in your soul, it is possible.

Now, for instance, where am I on the soul road map? I see a little person who is chugging along all by himself as usual to be better, but still very far away from full maturity, on a remote route which is not even paved by any religions. Although he had numerous chances to be exposed to quite a few different religions in life, he was not convinced by any. As a by-product, he has been able to keep an objective view.

FIFTEEN:

Doctrine of Heaven vs. Hell

A person dies. The body goes dead, and afterwards the soul escapes the body, for the soul is not dead but alive. If it were dead, it could not come out of the body on its own. Now we are left with one question. Where does the soul go? According to the whole big picture, the soul is examined for its maturity before it is either reincarnated into a new body or taken away forever to be inserted into an eternal body of a supreme being. Nonetheless, according to some religions, the soul goes initially to staging areas and ultimately either to heaven or to hell. Where are they located in the universe?

Have you ever wondered that the very place we live in can really be either heaven or hell? I have. Incidentally, I am convinced that our earth is either heaven or hell for us. Only hours ago, I drove on the sunny U.S. 101 freeway and cut through a quarter-mile-long gloomy shadow of cumulus. I really felt like going into hell from heaven and vice versa. They were all on the same freeway. Let's study three cases.

Case A: Once there was a continuous downpour for days and days here in the northern California. Houses were flooded in lower parts, and so many trees were toppled over. I opened up a newspaper and spotted an eye-catching photo. In it, two homeless persons were walking in the heavy rain. A young man was praying with hands together and a young woman was pushing a shopping cart filled with belongings.

Case B: Recently Prince William and Princess Kate of the British royal families have agreed to name their baby Charlotte Elizabeth Diana and stirred the whole world a bit. Speaking of Princess Diana, she appeared happy during her marriage, but she suffered a lot indeed due to bad marriage. She was followed and loved by practically the entire world. Nonetheless, she lived an unhappy life up until tragic death.

Case C: A greatly rich but lonely old man lived in a huge but dark house with his middle-aged son who caved in to get married only because it was his father's nagging wish. Through a matchmaker, a young lady agreed to move in for three weeks to live with them for a lucrative sum of money. She had to watch endless TV dramas with his father mostly. It was terrible, but she couldn't even get out of the contract.

In general, all three cases above are self-explanatory. As described clearly, heaven and hell are not located in two separate places. They are all geographically and physically positioned at one place in each case. Depending on facts or circumstances, only our soul should determine or judge the place to be either heaven or hell per se. Based on the logic, it could be interpreted that they solely exist within our soul.

In Case A, certainly, the young couple soaked in the cold rain with all their earthly belongings was experiencing one of the worst moments in their lifetime here on the earth. Despite of praying, they were dragging their feet inside hell. In the meantime, what about readers of the very newspaper? Some in heaven should have felt sad or even teared up, but others in hell themselves should have felt totally indifferent.

In Case B, obviously, Princess Diana was not happy in most of her marriage based on all the facts revealed later. Even though she had worldly popularity, symbolic prestige, envied wealth, and above all personal charm, nothing could be more crucial than her inner need for a true personal love. Accordingly, she appeared to reside in heaven, but she was actually struggling in hell. Personal happiness is important.

In Case C, basically, all the human beings are social animals. For most people, loneliness brings in unhappiness. The old man really wanted to turn his life around from hell to heaven by taking someone else into his house and he did. However, she ended up walking into hell, following money. Acting on my request for help, the supreme beings sent me this content in a telepathic dream received on May 13, 2015.

Years ago, I happened to meet a nice gentleman at a local car stereo shop. He was the owner. After taking care of the business, we engaged in a small talk on our daily life. Days later, he invited me over to his house to have a dinner. After the meal, I found myself in a group to study the Bible. They insisted that only the followers of their religion would go to heaven and all the others would end up in hell, period.

Contrary to a doctrine of a particular religion, either of heaven or hell is not designed or reserved for an afterlife. Every human being living a life here on the earth is situated either in heaven or in hell at every moment during an entire life. For real, each and every human being lives a life with ups and downs. The same could be interpreted as such that everyone must be going through heaven or hell all the time.

Certainly, a doctrine of heaven vs. hell set aside for afterlife does not work well with a doctrine of reincarnation that gives any immature soul another chance in a new body upon bodily death. Evidently, the Bible had both doctrines with conflicting soul plans. As such, the Second Council of Constantinople in 553 C.E. decided to strategically remove the doctrine of reincarnation from the Bible once and for all.

However, the Bible still seems to have a trace of the removed doctrine where it talked about the Second Coming. Jesus Christ allegedly promised to come back to his people. If so, his original soul should get into a new body since his original body would not be available after such a long time. Therefore, it wouldn't even be another resurrection for sure. In a nutshell, it would not be different from a reincarnation.

Going back to our original discussion on the subject, the supreme beings basically designed the human beings in a way that all of us would be on an emotional roller coaster to feel either heavenly or hellish depending on our soulness. What would make us realize that we are in heaven or in hell? Would it be happiness, money, both or neither one of them? I would explore its criteria by oversimplifying four nations.

First, in general, the United States of America must be considered as heaven since she gives so much happiness to so many warm-hearted people from diverse walks of life, has a ready access to so much money available in the world, and draws deeply soulistical people from all over the globe. Since the country has enough survival money to go around, money makes no difference. Happiness makes a difference.

Second, soulistically, most people in Nepal had felt that they resided in heaven since their awesome nature gave them so much happiness even though they had little money. However, when the big earthquakes hit the country in 2015, their heaven turned into hell immediately due to a loss of so many loved ones and a horrible destruction of their country. Fortunately, a virtual lack of looters flagged a fast recovery.

Third, too many people in affluent South Korea feel they are so unhappy. A towering suicide rate is a symptom. It may be due to a grave degree of mistrust in their societies. Superficial materialism is so rampant over genuine soulism. Prejudiced by perception, they may not grasp that the above negatives denote hell in a way. If not hell, why would they flock to so many churches to go to heaven at last after death?

Fourth, as of today on October 21, 2023, it is so sad that North Korea is still a pure hell. Except one, everybody fears an unjust sudden execution by state. It is not soulistic. Life precedes happiness. If so, none may realize what level of personal happiness is a norm for humans including them. Confined in the massive system of slavery with no freedom, their lowly survival is so precarious, lacking money as well.

In essence, happiness is the most important criterion between heaven and hell. Money is fairly important as well, but only up to a minimum amount for an adequate survival. Beyond that amount, money does not play a significant role. Now, if you were in heaven, would you smile? Yes, indeed. If you were in hell, would you cry? Yes, too bad. It is part of our instinct to rejoice in heaven and avoid hell if we can.

Hence, a fear factor against hell or purgatory due to agony of punishment exists right by a joy factor for heaven. Despite such human weakness, the Roman Catholic Church tolerated shameless pardoners selling dishonest indulgences for reducing or removing temporal punishment in purgatory. It was banned, but it triggered a reformation. Yet, a similar practice of forgiving past or future sins still exists from fear.

Supersonic airplanes can fly faster than the speed of sound. The supreme beings aboard a UFO can travel faster than the currently-known speed of light through wormholes, but they can't go faster than the speed of time. Nothing can. Light and time are not the same, let alone their travel speed. We can even play with physical properties of sound or light, but time is entirely different. Nothing can manipulate time.

Accordingly, a time machine is nothing but a fiction. In life, we commit a sin in an action or behavior within the confines of time. Thus time contains our action or behavior which in turn contains our sin. Our sin is contained in time. In actuality, no one can reverse time which contains our sin. By logic, no one can reverse our sin, either. Then forgiving, i.e., erasing or wiping out, of our sin is nothing but a fiction.

A practice to forgive sins upon faith-based salvation seems a mystical trick to fix a logical pitfall off the doctrine of heaven vs. hell, lacking the old doctrine of reincarnation. Many Christians do commit or repeat sins, believing God's forgiveness if asked. Anyone can talk about forgiving sins, but nobody including God or gods can reverse them, period. Can you now eat an apple eaten already or not on a tree yet?

Now, going one step further from exploring criteria for heaven and hell with respect to happiness, I should talk about happiness itself. Of course, it is so critical for heaven. Meanwhile, in a sense, success is associated with happiness, and failure is associated with sadness. However, depending on whose success or failure a case turns out to be, a person may feel heavenly or hellish in a uniquely piercing manner.

Given a failure, if it is yours and if you feel sad, you are in hell. If it is not yours and if you still feel sad, you are in heaven. If it is yours and if you feel no sadness, you are in heaven. If it is not yours and if you feel no sadness, you are in hell. Given a success, no matter who claims it, if you feel happy, you are in heaven. If you don't feel happy, you are in hell. In essence, your personal happiness dictates all.

As exposed in the above analysis of happiness itself, personal happiness is the most critical ingredient in making up any heaven for a person, household, community, society, country or world for that matter. Of course, not everybody in each group is always expected to feel personal happiness due to imperfect human nature. Perfection is impossible to achieve in nature. We would always have some exceptions.

Have you wondered why homeless people are found in the heavenly United States much like in the hellish North Korea? They suffer from financial and/or mental hardships due to a lack of family bonds along with inhumane societal system flaws demanding perfection. There are two types of the homeless. Some are coincidental while many are stuck. When the time comes, the former get out, but the latter stay.

Unlike the latter, the former can be helped by others easily for good. Any immature societies could even do that. Not easy, but all global societies must rescue the latter, too. By doing so, they would deliver heaven by way of personal happiness to the most helpless people being suffered in hell. The idea of handing over a piece of heaven to others is cool. It does not have to be in the form of money. Think about it.

Not just because he is a divine pope, but because he has a warm heart, I truly respect Pope Francis. In February 2015, he began to offer hot showers and neat haircuts to the homeless at St. Peter's Square within Vatican City, thereby sharing a cool piece of live heaven in his own sensitive way. Now, to do the same, let's pick up all the litter. To be more mature, let's not litter. The supreme beings are watching us.

SIXTEEN:

The Art of Reincarnation

Our soul survives our body since it is not disposable. Differing from our body, our soul carries an invisible frame. It is not subject to wear and tear even during a multiple use. Unlike the well-known religious doctrine of heaven vs. hell, a technique of reincarnation employs that no soul of ours is of a single use. Consequently, not a single soul gets thrown away, like into hell forever, once manufactured at a factory. Besides, a single human life span is too short for any of our brand-new souls to obtain full maturity for heaven, thereby falling into hell if only the doctrine of heaven vs. hell is true.

What is reincarnation? It is simply a factual process in which a yet-immature or not-fully-mature-yet soul would be inserted into a brand-new human body being readied in a womb as a fetus with a sufficiently-developed brain so that the soul should go through another completely different life on the earth to get more mature while experiencing all sorts of daily matters until death according to the supreme beings.

Now, what is incarnation? It is the same process as the above except that a brand-new thus blank or empty soul newly-manufactured over there and transported to the earth by the supreme beings in a UFO would be used instead of a used thus a little or substantially mature soul just picked up so that the soul should taste the very first life on the earth to get mature before the next according to the supreme beings.

As a result, a person with an incarnated soul should display an extremely immature attitude up to a certain point in his or her life before starting to get serious about living a meaningful life here on the earth. Keep in mind that such a person had to begin his or her first life with a zero maturity. Depending on a lifestyle formed with a distinct personality, everybody moves on a maturity scale at his or her own pace.

Well, what happens to a fully mature soul picked up and examined by the supreme beings in a UFO? They take it to their planet to insert it into a newly-manufactured body so that a brand-new supreme being with a fully mature soul should become a permanent member of their eternal society. Surely, all the supreme beings live forever. They don't die. Hence, their fully mature soul could rarely leave their body.

Realistically, the above is the case with virtually no exception. The supreme beings hardly commit suicide, kill each other or even volunteer to be killed by their system so that their fully mature soul could return to the earth in order to be inserted into a human body in a reincarnation process. Meantime, even the supreme beings can be killed in natural disasters, but any such victim's soul will be consumed there.

In other words, there is absolutely no chance for any fully mature souls already being used in their eternal world to come back to the earth in the form of a freestanding soul. According to the enlightenment materials received from the supreme beings through the telepathic mail on July 7, 2006, they all had a final option open to return before an insertion. They could've come back initially, declining an eternal life.

As explained so far, the tradition of reincarnation is in the center of all the principles and procedures on how the universal life system works regarding the whole big picture. However, only our human souls go through a reincarnation process after our bodily death. All the spirits possessed by all the living things on the earth do not go through the same process simply because they perish upon their bodily death.

Therefore, contrary to a common belief proclaimed by certain religions such as Buddhism for example, animals as well as insects do not possess a reincarnated human soul. Repeatedly speaking, they do possess not a soul but a spirit. The same applies to all our pets like cats, dogs, and so forth. As a result, Buddhist monks in their mistaken belief refrain from killing animals or insects. They only kill plants to eat.

In fact, if you visit Buddhist temples, you'll see that nearly all the monks are vegetarians or even vegans. Based on their stern religious dogmas, they only use grains, fruits, and vegetables for a meal day after day for years and years. Such a unique practice was caused by a limited knowledge in the partial big picture exposed to the enlightened Buddha. He himself at first ate meat. In confusion, he later refrained.

Mainly due to the same reason, although Siddhartha Gautama founded Buddhism based on a telepathic mail that he received from the supreme beings while he prayed under a big tree in India, the religion like other religions could not offer correct factual answers to our most baffling questions with regards to origin, purpose of life, and final destination of soul after reincarnations for the human beings in general.

Not only Shakyamuni Buddha but also his followers were kept in the dark for thousands of years from their start. Instead of pursuing answers to the above for the betterment of humankind, most monks wasted a lifetime just to train or up their body and soul by chanting, meditating, praying, etc. Even so, the supreme beings were silent because the human beings were not ready at all to receive the whole big picture.

By design, it is purely natural for the human beings to kill some animals or insects except for all our lovely pets for actual survival, satisfying nutritional or medicinal needs. In fact, all those living things including plants were brought here by the supreme beings for the sake of keeping us alive. Incurable diseases can be solved by exploring them in order to resolve a root cause rather than just peripheral symptoms.

Except to satisfy our survivalist consumption needs, the human beings are not supposed to kill any living things. Can you identify an animal, insect, monad or plant that kills others beyond survivalist consumption needs? Perhaps not. Only human beings kill all the living things including each other at will for all sorts of regretful and ridiculous reasons such as emotion, fun, money, prejudice, pride, religion, etc.

If you noticed, as you get more mature, you become less inclined to kill any living things including small insects. You develop a certain level of respect toward others as well as your environments in which all the living things survive. Actually, even your tiniest behavior or mind-set in treating others, whether living or not, illustrates your maturity level. The supreme beings in charge of you are watching you 24/7.

The more you get mature, the less you get conscious of their watch. This precipitates success in maturing a soul to the fullest in multiple reincarnations, letting it experience different life encounters as a blank or empty soul gets to be fully mature for its prospective usage. Human religions are a good tool to boost our maturity as long as they are helpful, but there're too many problems due to subjectivity involved.

A living proof of such a typical human phenomenon lies with an apparent existence of numerous denominations or sects for virtually all of the modern religions on the earth. In fact, the whole chaotic religious scene was purely caused by a lack of access to the whole big picture by the founders. Hence, human creativity or subjectivity had to be employed in order to get around, thereby resulting in illogical dogmas.

Aside from religions, politics are a good tool as well to improve our maturity level as long as a political machine provides an ideal system to people in a geographical region. Historically speaking, a clear majority of the human beings involved in politics has made so many errors in inventing a suitable political system primarily due to blindly relying on our human creativity and subjectivity, leading to confusions.

What should be an antonym for democracy? Due to an unfortunate global brainwash in modern times, it should be quite easy for anyone to mention communism to answer. For your information, communism should not be a political system. Instead, it should be an economic system in which all the earnings are distributed equally to people regardless of individual contributions to a communal production effort.

Apparently, communism and democracy don't even belong to the same category. A correct answer to the above question should be dictatorship. Since they are in the same category, democracy and dictatorship could be compared to each other objectively with a definite result that democracy is superior to dictatorship. Hence, democracy thrives today in most mature countries as opposed to immature countries.

Now, what should be an antonym for capitalism? It should be communism as illustrated in the above. Because both terms are in the same category for an economic system, they could be compared to each other objectively, resulting in a productive assessment that capitalism is far superior to communism. Thus, capitalism thrives wildly today even in China with communism that shouldn't be a political system.

Exactly, what has happened or what is happening to all those countries which adopted communism as a political system by making an obvious judgment error in a sense that communism is actually an economic system doomed to fail? In terms of their economic system, communism was proven to be no match against capitalism. In addition, communism as a political system also proved to be absolutely worthless.

For real, if a country adopts a political system from a wrong category, it'll fail. How about adopting a political system from a category of religious system? Politics do not mix well with religions. Analyze the Middle East including a Jewish state or many others. Are they peaceful? No way. For peace, altruism must reign in international relations, too. For our new world, end should not justify the means, period.

Let's imagine that you build a nation in an area with people from all over the globe. Given a freedom, they will adopt democracy over dictatorship as a political system and capitalism over communism as an economic system, period. Forget socialism. Woven in everywhere to a certain degree, it is an economic redistribution concept mistaken as system. Religions would play no roles because they are too divisive.

Going back to the original subject, I would clear up procedural matters with regard to the reincarnation process. Aside from all sorts of UFOs, even the human beings could produce stealth aircrafts that could evade our earthly radars. However, could the stealth airplanes evade our human eyes as well all the time? No, not likely. We could see anything including UFOs if they're at certain speeds within our sight.

Per historical artifacts or written records, the human beings from all walks of life have spotted all sorts of UFOs everywhere on the earth even in ancient times to nowadays. UFOs maneuvered by the supreme beings fly above us 24/7. They usually move too fast for us to spot. We can see them if they slow down to suck in souls like a vacuum cleaner to assess them or stay afloat to insert them into human fetuses.

The supreme beings must have sent down the above vacuum cleaner concept to me in a quick telepathic thought as I was waking up on May 24, 2015. I requested their help with this page while I was getting into bed the night before, but not a single train of thought on reincarnation was in me the morning after. In essence, a vacuum cleaner could suck in more dust particles only if you move it over them slowly.

It neatly explains a geographical shift and a time lag between two consecutive lives of a soul being reincarnated. If a live soul escapes from a dead body, it goes up in the air. Whenever it feels ready for another life, it goes to a certain aerial spot that is good for being sucked into a passing UFO. During a voluntary stage of being in-between, it reflects on his or her own self to be a desirable for the supreme beings.

Of course, the supreme beings do exercise a certain level of preference over handpicking a select batch of souls either to be harvested or to be reincarnated. The rest would be thrown back out to the air to process more self-reflection. What kind of a soul is not desirable for the supreme beings? A soul of a person who committed suicide or took a human life for any reason is most awful. A life is not ours to waste.

SEVENTEEN:
Human Ethics and Morals

Nearly all the human beings grapple with ethics and morals on a daily basis. Nobody could be always righteous, for our soul is not perfect, thus making all sorts of mistakes. How about the supreme beings? Since they all have a fully mature soul although imperfect, they seldom combat ethical or moral problems. Then, it becomes obvious that ethics or morals play a clandestine role to improve our maturity, for we could always learn from our immature mistakes as well. In other words, human ethics and morals are a transitional tool designed to assist us for full maturity by trial and error.

Ethics and morals are similar, but they are different. Human ethics are related to our external action, behavior or conduct and often mandated by social norms. They change, too, as a society changes. On the other hand, human morals are connected to our internal conscience which tries to deal with objective principles and subjective interpretations over right from wrong. They haven't changed in human history.

Human ethics or morals are a marvelously complex and helplessly sensitive subject since they could be affected by our emotion which could rule our reasoning rather easily. For instance, there's a thought-provoking romantic scene in the delightful 1987 Hollywood film 'Moonstruck' in which Ronny sweeps Loretta off her feet by saying that people are imperfect unlike snowflakes or stars and to ruin themselves.

On their intimate turmoil that followed in the movie, it's such that no one could dare to blame either one of them for their immature affair perhaps because we are all human. Ethically or morally, all the human beings are so vulnerable. For instance, there is a catchy scene in the 1988 Hollywood film 'The Last Temptation of Christ' in which no one dares to stone a sinned lady upon a righteous demand from Jesus.

Quite realistically portrayed in the impressive scene, Jesus Christ himself picks up stones in hands to calm down an emotional crowd, but he just uses them to make his point. Theoretically, he could not have thrown them to her, either. He was also an imperfect human being like everybody else. He knew very well that only a perfect god should judge her. Incidentally, the supreme beings don't judge humans, either.

Have you seen any human body alive without a soul? Have you found any human soul that seems always perfect? Have you met any human being who never tells a single lie? Have you discovered any person who always acts righteous? Undoubtedly, all the answers should be decisively negative. Why? Everyone has a soul, every soul is imperfect, no one is always honest, and furthermore everyone makes mistakes.

Apparently, human quality exposed above seems to be quite problematic, but ironically our daily life gets more challenging and interesting since we live in a chaotic world where we need to deal with our own ethical or moral issues in addition to interacting with others with similar problems. What would be real reasons behind all the human dilemmas in processing personal situations involving ethics or morals?

When the supreme beings created the human beings, they exercised an exquisite touch in designing our body and soul in a way that both elements should be needed to form a life. A body alone can never live a life. Neither can a soul. Whether a body or a person for that matter is alive or not is determined by a presence of a soul inside of a body because a soul never dies. When a person dies, his or her body dies.

Meanwhile, a soul cannot go into a body on its own while a soul can escape a body on its own after a body dies. In fact, a soul can only get into a body when it gets inserted by the supreme beings into a freshly-developing embryo or fetus with a sufficiently-grown brain which is fully ready to accommodate or receive a soul. Once it happens, a fetus is genuinely turned into a human being with a body and a soul.

Until it happens, a fetus is absolutely without a soul. Thus it is not a human being yet even though it may exhibit a sign of wriggling body parts triggered by a pumping heart. In fact, such a sign of action indicates a presence of a spirit that gets activated only by blood being circulated in a body. By the way, a spirit becomes alive when a body gets to live by a pumping heart and a spirit goes dead when a body dies.

As illustrated, a presence of a spirit in a body can be evidenced with a heart pumping blood into other body parts. Meanwhile, a presence of a soul can be detected by a brain activity, however small, that is physiologically observed by EEG showing brain waves including bursts made by a soul passing a network of neurons activated by circulating blood. Conclusively, a heart gets a spirit before a brain gets a soul.

Given all the related facts above, we can technically pinpoint an exact time of a fetus turning into a human being, thereby effectively ending a constant debate over abortions. Killing a soulless fetus is an artificial abortion, but killing a fetus with a soul is a murder, for it is a de facto or bona fide human being. The former stays in a realm of human ethics and morals, but the latter steps into a criminal law territory.

Besides, the latter action clearly negates an insertion work methodically performed earlier by the supreme beings. On the other hand, the former action does not interfere with efforts of the supreme beings although it kills a living thing. Well, wasting a female egg in menstruation or male sperms in ejaculation produces no guilt since it is a natural process. Yet, terminating an unborn embryo or fetus is another story.

Anatomically speaking, it is inevitable that we have so many ethical or moral issues dealt on an individual basis, which are germane to human combination of body and soul. As briefly touched upon before, a warm heart exerts a spirit which stimulates an animalistic action, behavior or conduct while a cool brain sparks a soul which galvanizes a godlike rationale, creating a conflict between behaving and thinking.

However, since a human soul is immature by nature, it readily succumbs to a spirit carrying out a bodily demand. In reality, although a perfect god exists in a corner of a soul, its power of persuasion for righteousness is quite minuscule. Thus, most ethical or moral mishaps are explained logically. Further, there is a physiological reality that a heart supplies blood to a brain as well, which means a direct manipulation.

If a sexual arousal begins to take place, blood tends to concentrate in sexual organs, making a penile erection or a vaginal excitement upon erection of female breast nipples. If then, where does an extra amount of blood originate from? It comes from a remote end of our body, i.e., our brain that uses a significant amount of blood, thereby minimizing our thinking power exerted by a soul coping with far less blood.

Physiology explains why humans easily succumb to bodily sexual appeals especially in extramarital love affairs. We are imperfect unlike gods, for our body can control soul. If so, it is against nature to require a straitjacket in sexuality. Besides, they have designed a human sexual intercourse as a clever means of reproduction for a success of a soul farm. Our ethics or morals dictate whether or not it is meaningful.

Aside from a physical or sexual attraction exhibited by a set of body mates, i.e., a female body and a male body, we exhibit another magnetic tendency in constantly seeking a soul mate fitly from the opposite sex. What is a soul mate? According to the supreme beings, if a perfect sheet of paper is torn off by hands into two, each piece is imperfect with a jagged edge. A soul mate is like a perfectly matching piece.

It's why a human soul is imperfect as well as utterly immature at the start of the very first incarnated earthly life. Like a whole unisex body, the supreme beings manufacture a whole unisex soul, but it is totally blank or empty with no content. So, they cut it off into two female and male pieces with a respective generic perfect god embedded in each one, and match each with a female or male fetus during insertion.

Accordingly, it is only natural for the human beings to constantly look for the other matching piece of their soul. In reality, it is just like trying to find a needle in a haystack, but we're programmed in a way to believe that it is possible. As a result, most human beings would keep trying till death. This fully explains earthly date, marriage, and affair scenes. In the process, we may encounter ethical or moral problems.

What happens to a set of torn-apart souls eventually? If they could not find or meet each other to consummate on the earth, they could ultimately rejoin as a perfect couple of the supreme beings in order to enjoy an eternal life together. It happens with completing multiple life cycles successfully. If one finishes earlier than the other, the one will wait until later in order to be a perfect couple with fully mature souls.

Going back to our original discussion on the subject of the human ethics and morals, learning invaluable lessons from all kinds of mistakes that the human beings are bound to make until death counts in moving up on a maturity scale. Besides a perfect god, only each individual involved should judge whether his or her certain action, behavior or conduct is humanly ethical or unethical as well as moral or immoral.

Consequently, it becomes quite critical that all of us must learn how to extend an honest apology to ourselves or to others if a contrition, regret, remorse or repentance is felt. In turn, only our internal or external disposition afterwards could affect a maturity level in terms of moving up or down. Well, each and every body part must serve a useful purpose. By washing hair, we can make fingertips clean for example.

By the same token, human arms are long enough to touch own genitalia with own hands, which serve as sexual orgasm organs besides just reproductive and urinary organs. In other words, by design, we have all the tools to go either way while haggling with our own ethical or moral dilemma. For this very reason, our human history either interpersonal or personal is full of people said to be unethical or immoral.

Due to misjudgment, there are still certain countries underdeveloped and some areas even in advanced countries, which treat personal moral issues like adultery for example as a crime on their book although not aggressively enforced, which can be punished by a prison term or a death sentence. It just goes to show that how a lot of human beings are still very confused about the whole business of ethics or morals.

Of course, I am not an exception, either, in the area of ethics and morals. Throughout my short life on the earth, I have made so many immature mistakes like everyone else. Amazingly, I had two consecutive telepathic dreams on this very delicate subject in the wee hours of February 16, 2015. First, I worried about being embarrassed for talking straight. Second, I quit driving and walked down from a scary curve.

In fact, as soon as I opened up my eyes at 5:39 a.m., I seriously started to ponder upon quitting on this very book. A puddle of cold sweat made me see what I was up against. Soon, a constant sharp pain suddenly began in my abdomen. As if I knew what it was, I requested the supreme beings to give me time to consider my options. It went away at once. A friend of mine made me feel that it was a test on my will.

Based on brave, critical, timely, unbiased, and wise thoughts exerted by the above nonreligious thoughtful soul, I saw myself leaning toward this crazy extraterrestrial book although I might be subject to all sorts of public laughs and ridicules extended from people with no factual information. After a serious debate with my own self, I came up with my own conclusion that it was imperative to save our humanity.

If I can add a final point to human ethics and morals, as far as my observation on the writing project is concerned, the supreme beings clearly wanted me to deal with this very complex subject in a separate chapter as what I have chosen. Oddly enough, although my late aunt was extremely ethical or moral in almost every aspect of her life, surely by design, I missed them totally in citing 20 good qualities of her soul.

EIGHTEEN:

Enlightenment Content (1)

Around 2:20 a.m. on July 7, 2006, I got knocked off the bed in my sleep and flung to the floor several feet away by a streak of kinetic energy like a powerful lightning strike. I was totally confused, but shocked that I did receive a huge volume of extraterrestrial knowledge materials in my brain. What? It was the enlightenment. How? Over 7 years later, I learned that the supreme beings utilized a telepathic mail. Whether wanted or not, it can happen to anybody anywhere anytime anyhow in ingeniously conspicuous ways. It is just a cognitive process of internalizing brand-new information.

Had I prepared myself in any fashion so that I could get enlightened in life ultimately? I had never even visited monasteries or temples to study with Christian or Buddhist monks nor had I been to a deep mountain in America, Tibet, India, Korea, etc. to meditate or pray for my enlightenment. I had been far from any ascetic spiritual endeavor, let alone being enlightened with extraterrestrial knowledge materials.

I was born in 1954 to an affluent household in Seoul. My mother from the north, who was a half Korean, met my father in the south soon after the tragic Korean War paused. However, my life turned upside down twice at ages 4 and 7 when my father abandoned us for Hong Kong and when my mother abandoned me for the U.S.A. They all disappeared. My aunt rescued me right before I was sent to an orphanage.

Although she was dirt poor herself, my aunt did not hesitate to take me under her wing. I only learned later that my father sent enough child support money regularly to my mother, but she sent us only a little due to her own situation. Actual sums received were not only so menial but also very few and far between. So I grew up poor, but I did not mind a constant poverty, for my aunt gave me her unlimited love.

By design, she allowed me a complete autonomy in making decisions on just about any personal situations ever since she began to raise me so that I could develop my own sense of confident and thoughtful navigation skill in my life. For instance, when I decided to study philosophy in college, she supported my lonely decision despite of no job prospect. Even my teachers worried for me upon hearing my decision.

Now, I'll talk about my own enlightenment content. Even though I did my best in jotting down everything that I could pull out from my instant memory almost immediately after I was suddenly hit with the extraterrestrial knowledge materials, I could only grasp a tiny portion of the materials in writing, compared to the entire volume transmitted to me and initially received by a subconscious section of my brain.

Accordingly, I have experienced over the years ever since that I already kind of know quite naturally a lot about the supreme beings, their lifestyles, and their environments. Whenever I would have an urge depending on a need to get deeper into any issue within the materials, certain pertinent information pieces would come up in my mind quite clearly as though they were coming out of distant memory of mine.

Of course, due to my mental or physical limitations as a human being, I could be completely or partially wrong on anything and everything that I would like to convey you in a random order, recapping all my enlightenment content which the supreme beings wanted me to retain for a reason. Logically speaking, I could be completely or partially right as well on anything and everything. The judgment is yours.

My enlightenment procedure was factual but surreal. It seemed like that all the pages were ripped right out of an entire set of the Encyclopedia Britannica and thrown at me one by one all within a second. Out of the countless pieces of information, I could only physically salvage my notes of 16 pages written in English or Korean with some drawings, which were prepared on four intermittent days in July 2006.

Fortunately, my notes that I could jot down focused quite heavily on the origin of the human beings on the earth based on the context of the universal life system operations. In fact, my first note of 7 pages prepared between 2:20 a.m. and 5:20 a.m. on July 7, 2006, recorded a title 'The Origin'. At this point in time, it is only my conjecture, but probably I chose to focus on the origin since it was most critical to us.

Now, I would step into fascinating details present in the extraterrestrial knowledge materials handed over to me by the supreme beings during the brief enlightenment event. However, I could only describe them from my perspectives limited by my own knowledge base and language capability. In other words, in delivering any new core concepts to you, I should rely on some earthly information as well if needed.

1. Oddly, global warming is the very first item that is recorded on my notes, but there is a perfect reason which will be corroborated in a little while as to why it was put in. I was a bit confused until later, but it became quite obvious that the supreme beings were not talking about our modern manmade global warming. Instead, they were referring to a natural global warming that had occurred in the olden days.

2. Global warming created a climate change on the earth, triggered a series of torrential rains in North America, flooded the whole Grand Canyon area making the Colorado River filled with so much water, and mistakenly attracted a UFO looking for a fertile land adjacent to a big river so that a frozen young white couple like Romeo and Juliet eloping from another soul farm could start a brand-new civilization.

3. The UFO looked similar to the one that I actually ran into on Monterey Road in San Jose, California, in 1984. The supreme beings safely landed their UFO on a riverside, but the very spot happened to be right below a vertical cliff. Some of them got off the vehicle to explore the area nearby. At the very moment, there was a big unexpected earthquake. It triggered a terrible landslide covering up the landing spot.

4. It was attributable to the careless supreme beings with fully mature but imperfect souls. They parked it there. In fact, sometimes they can't avoid natural disasters, either. Hence, the entire craft with the still-frozen human beings as well as all crew members of the supreme beings in or out of the UFO was buried deep at the basis of a triangular mound with a steep slope around somewhere in the Grand Canyon.

5. Thousands of years must have passed since then. The landslide spot might not be located currently right next to the Colorado River itself perhaps because the river could have receded down or changed its course of flow since then. At any rate, the Romeo and Juliet along with their souls are still well-kept fully frozen in a container which can only be thawed with solar energy after being exposed under the sun.

6. The young white couple who could have been an Adam and Eve in North America if everything had worked out as planned before was in a serious love relationship, but their respective parents never approved their consummation. They requested the supreme beings for a soul farm transfer. A goal congruence test was met. They got transported here. However, all of them got buried alive under the dirt mound.

7. Given the fact that all the supreme beings live an eternal life in the universe with absolutely no such essential body needs as clothing, food, oxygen, sex, sleep, water, etc., they could be still alive there either inside or outside of the UFO. As such, once detected and uncovered by the human beings with proper heavy equipment to carefully remove all the dirt, they could finally go or be taken back to their place.

8. Although my notes don't indicate precisely when, the first discovery and the second discovery are duly noted. The former is by Indians with an x mark and the latter is by whites and Asians with an exclamation mark. They're very clear, but what do they mean? Based on my interpretations, they were partially exposed by Indians in the past, but they were buried back. As such, they wait for whites and Asians.

9. In order to substantiate the fact that the supreme beings brought the human beings and all other living things to the earth after creating all the original species elsewhere, my notes tell that Charles Darwin's evolutionism is entirely misguided as evidenced by fossils of most species suddenly appearing in the Cambrian Period and that they transported adults, babies, and seeds of the species to the earth in UFOs.

10. In addition, there is a mention that the supreme beings operate a DNA or gene bank like the Noah's Ark to preserve all the species that they create for their soul farms. With regard to preserving the species, all the human beings also play an important role by producing offspring naturally while contributing to a prosperous growth of the soul farms. We're here to get more mature by mixing our blood. What?

11. The supreme beings operate many soul farms in the universe to meet their practical demand on fully mature souls to be used with their manufactured bodies. In the past, a nasty human space war broke out among three soul farms on adjacent planets. A single race of black, white or brown armed with space weapons like laser, nukes, etc. resided on each farm. All three planets were destroyed beyond repairs.

12. The supreme beings stepped in and stopped the apocalyptic war, but it was too late. As a remedy for racial peace out of the box, their association agreed to experiment for a unified race on a remote planet named by us the earth. They brought all initial humans here on soul farm transfers. Consequently, the supreme beings worry about weapons of mass destruction owned and operated by the human beings.

13. Due to a bad memory about the Colorado River, the supreme beings naturally avoided North America per se and brought another set of white human beings way later to a stretch between two rivers of the Tigris and the Euphrates. In the middle of three continents, the area was an excellent choice to mix blood among races within the human species. Blood mixing with other species isn't designed to be viable.

14. Amazingly, the supreme beings reminded us to realize that absolutely no transitional forms or species exist on the earth or on any similar planets in the whole universe for that matter between chimpanzees and the human beings. This is why we do not see chimpanzees talking like humans. It proves that we're not a product of evolution but a product of creation. The invisible gods did not create us. They did.

15. So soon after failing the Colorado River project, the supreme beings tried to plant a new set of white human beings atop the rugged Andes Mountains in South America. This time, there was no major river. As such, their Andean project was doomed to be evaporated since all those thirsty humans had to disperse all over frantically to look for water. Tragically, most failed to find it and perished rather quickly.

16. Without breathable air and drinkable water, the human beings shall not survive. Air is commonly abundant everywhere on the earth, but water is never. Hence, all four major ancient human civilizations developed close to rivers, i.e., the Egyptian around the Nile River, the Mesopotamian between the Tigris and Euphrates Rivers, the Indus near the Indus River, and the Far East not far from the Yellow River.

17. The supreme beings delivered brown race to the Yellow River area, white race to the area around the Tigris and Euphrates Rivers, and black race to the Nile River area. They never brought anyone directly to the Indus River area. People from all areas of the Yellow, Tigris, Euphrates, and Nile Rivers migrated to the area. White people migrated to the Nile River area also to scatter black people everywhere.

18. From current offspring headcounts populated in different parts of the earth soul farm, retroactively applying a respective population growth rate adjusted by factors like climate, culture, disaster, disease, famine, history, war, etc., a reverse calculation could be made in order to confirm the above arrival sequence for three races of the human beings. Arrival? Our original ancestors were arrived at a soul farm.

NINETEEN:

Enlightenment Content (2)

I have two points. First, upon completing Items 3 to 6 for the previous chapter, I felt a chill with awe and found myself shivering a while even though it was summer. I was indeed doing something positive for all the supreme beings. Second, when I was thinking about making the above point in this paragraph while driving on the freeway shortly after midnight on June 11, 2015, I heard an extremely loud bang, which was deafening like a bomb explosion, striking a right rear of my car. Puzzled over no damages, I concluded that it was their telepathic thunder approving my line of thought.

19. To my surprise, the supreme beings even touch upon a perennial subject of logic vs. religion as spelled out clearly in a corner of my notes written at my enlightenment. Our logic survives on rationality with a reasoning power to provide a persuasive rationale. To the contrary, our current earthly religions are largely based on illogic with dogmatic mystery which creates ambiguity, frustration, and nonsense.

20. As such, our logical mind cannot accommodate mysterious religions, and dogmatic religions cannot tolerate a logical soul. Apparently, they are at odds with each other. Meanwhile, so as to improve maturity of the human beings, the supreme beings point out a remedial fact of our life that a practical tool to use in solving fundamental human issues is not current earthly religions but a logical mind or religion.

21. All the human beings use one or more different languages to communicate with other humans. A language consists of both or either one of spoken sounds and written letters. It is nothing but a communication tool adopted by a group of people. It does not call for prerequisite equipment. It is very easy for the human beings to create or modify one. Most of all, anyone can learn to use it with conscious effort.

22. The supreme beings have designed us to require a womb to get nurtured before birth. There is no exception. Hence, they brought us here on the earth as adults or babies. If babies had no adults around to learn an existing language, they had to invent a brand-new language while growing up. It explains why we see so many different earthly languages. Meantime, some of our languages came from other planets.

23. So as to convey an importance of fact over truth, the supreme beings reminded us a very well-known case of a flat earth vs. a spherical earth. Despite some people who asserted for the latter as being a truth, historically speaking, our ancient through medieval societies mistakenly believed the former as being a truth since its fact was never available. Truth could change anytime while fact would never change.

24. A blank piece of paper is two-dimensional, but it exists in a three-dimensional space. Any point marked or any line drawn on one side of the paper cannot see the other side of the paper or space for that matter. However, if you make a gaping hole through the point or line, the other side gets to be seen as well by the very point or line on one side. What was on their mind presenting the above example to us?

25. The supreme beings wanted us to realize clearly that we the human beings possess a three-dimensional body, but in actuality we exist in a four-dimensional space as well as living in a three-dimensional world. Although we could not see the other side of a four-dimensional space, we could still see anything from such a space, i.e., UFOs for instance. Also, we might get to keep any UFO as evidence if allowed.

26. Speaking of the two human beings who are still buried under a spot in the Grand Canyon in North America, once they are discovered and unfrozen eventually, they are like immigrants to their new planet. They are fully capable of learning any earthly languages such as English at school. In addition, they could even teach us the universal language. Their portable language translator is inside the UFO as well.

27. The universal language mentioned above means one and only communication means used in the universe by all sorts of living things except for the human beings on the earth and other soul farms. In a nutshell, it means telepathy. It also means that those two female and male human beings trapped alive but frozen underneath a triangular dirt mound have a fully functional telepathic capability for some reason.

28. To my amazement, my notes taken immediately after the dramatic enlightenment event go further into more fascinating details such that they were even trained on how to operate parts of the very UFO just in case for the journey, that they could also directly communicate with the supreme beings handling their case in the universe by telepathy, and that nuclear and solar hybrid energy powered the very UFO.

29. The human beings in a three-dimensional world may believe that the earth is so many light-years away from all the stars or their planets. The supreme beings possess a drastically different view of the same universe because they pass through wormholes to reduce any space travel distance to a realistic level in actual terms. Simply because they can do so, we believe them to be from a four-dimensional space.

30. If you think about it carefully given the fact that the supreme beings transport all the initial human beings as well as all the other living things to their soul farms located in numerous corners of the whole universe all the time, the human beings also exist in the same four-dimensional space. In other words, the universe is the universe. In fact, there is no other universe away from the universe in which we exist.

31. Figuratively speaking, they brought six souls in six human bodies to instigate the earth soul farm according to the supreme beings. If so, there were two human beings, i.e., a female and a male, from each of three available races, i.e., black, white or brown. By any measure, the earth soul farm operation has proven to be extremely successful so far in terms of an overall population growth over a short period.

32. If that is the case, a question remains. Since the human beings produce only their bodies among themselves through a sexual intercourse and a consequential pregnancy, where have billions of additional souls except for the initial six souls come from? My enlightenment notes clearly spell out that the supreme beings transported each and every one of them to the earth in their UFOs after being manufactured.

33. The notes also mention a recycling aspect of all the souls as well. In other words, a soul is reincarnated into another new human body getting readied in a female womb once it gets out of a dead body and it is not fully mature yet. Accordingly, the supreme beings normally have to bring to the earth only the incremental souls needed for a net growth. Incidentally, a soul is shapeless, volumeless, and weightless.

34. The supreme beings flown in UFOs come to the earth all the time to produce enough fully mature souls fast. This explains why all shapes of UFOs have been spotted by the human beings all over the globe since the ancient times. Occasionally, they carry out a drastic measure like planting a horrible virus such as AIDS, bird flu, SARS and others to control or stimulate a certain segment of earthly population.

35. According to the supreme beings, the earth has virtually all the species for the living things such as humans, animals, insects, monads, and plants present in the universe. In fact, they have brought all the species created and found in the universe to the earth soul farm. This corroborates the point that no transitional species between chimpanzees and the human beings are found on the earth and in the universe.

36. There is a valid reason why most UFOs are also called flying saucers because they possess a spherical body shape with a circular wing in the middle. They're designed to afford a very fast rotation if necessary during their flight. According to my enlightenment notes, such a rotation helps them to make consecutive sharp turns at a very short notice. However, only their shell rotates. Their cabin never rotates.

37. UFOs can fly faster than a known speed of light. However, it still takes them a while to finish a trip in space due to a sheer size of the universe. As such, it is important to carry on board as little supplies as possible for soul farm transfer. It is partly why the human beings are frozen alive before their soul leaves their body. Their often-naked body never takes in food, oxygen or water, but their soul is intact.

38. In fact, a soul within a brain can be frozen with a body. The same soul can be totally revitalized with intact memory when the same body gets unfrozen no matter when. Meanwhile, a duplicate soul can slip out of a body during a dream period, wander around the so-called parallel universe, and get back in right before the dream ends. Such a dream is bound to be forgotten in a flash unlike a real-life memory.

39. Each and every soul possessed by all the human beings was initially transported here by the supreme beings. It was newly manufactured, used or being used right before a respective incarnation, reincarnation or soul farm transfer. Basically all of the souls get inserted into a fetus in a womb, but some of them get inserted into a person either by design or by mistake so as to cause a multiple personality disorder.

40. An unfaltering population growth in a soul farm for any particular species including the human beings poses a serious issue for survival due to inevitable food shortages. According to the concerned supreme beings, each soul farm can afford only up to a certain number of the human beings. There will be a saturation point in the future no matter what. It is why the supreme beings keep creating a new soul farm.

41. Coincidentally, it is also why the human beings keep exploring the space to search for a feasible planet and establish a human colony there. Mars project is an example. However, based on the whole big picture regarding how the universal life system works, it will never work at all, period. Most of all, even if people go to Mars, how can they have a child successfully with inability to insert a soul into a fetus?

42. Besides the ultimate human goal above, there is none other in looking for any sign of life in the outer space. If so, what is wrong with an idea to establish such a remote self-sufficient colony or settlement in the middle of a desert which already has a plenty of air except for food and water? Due to human ingenuity, no global food shortages exist yet. Hence, all the regional famines are a result of poor logistics.

43. Going back to the world of the supreme beings, they manage their own means of personal communications, i.e., telepathy, which works equivalent to a human language. Although there are no regional political units such as nation or state with own geographical borders, they tend to belong to certain functional communities in which they all vote for critical decisions on their own version of a wireless internet.

44. Speaking of a wireless technology, according to my enlightenment notes, the supreme beings even transport electrical energy from one point to another point wirelessly after producing electricity from nuclear or solar power cells. Personally, I witnessed twice, i.e., in 1984 on the first UFO with flickering lights and in 2014 on another big UFO with projecting lights, that they were actually utilizing electricity.

45. All the supreme beings have a fully mature but imperfect soul after all. As such, they can commit a serious mistake, too, sometimes. Even so, there is no death penalty. Instead, they can be voted to a remote soul farm with harsh reality to carry out a set of dreary tasks while rehabilitating. On the other hand, for a superb behavior, they can be voted to a nice area of a soul farm to appear in a live reality show.

46. Lastly, an invisible generic perfect god exists in each soul of all the human and supreme beings. Meanwhile, much like us, the supreme beings possess a visible physical body which is subject to a planetary gravity in the universe. As such, they also will float in the space with a zero gravity. However, in order to stabilize their posture during the flight, they wear shoes on electromagnetic floor onboard the UFO.

TWENTY:

A Space Game of Triball

Two days after the enlightenment event, I happened to watch the 2006 World Cup soccer final match of Italy vs. France on TV from 11:00 a.m. to 1:30 p.m. on July 9, 2006. Watching the exciting game in which Italy won over France in a penalty shootout by 5:3, I realized that I had spotted in the enlightenment content a unique ball game played by the supreme beings with no sorcery moves made on the ground. It was like our soccer, but each game required three teams. Depending on situations or strategies, anyone of two other teams could turn into a friend, adding complexity to a game.

On the earth, most human beings enjoy, i.e., play or watch, many unique ball games such as baseball, basketball, football, pool, soccer, table tennis, tennis, volleyball, etc. to accept challenge, discipline body, have fun or make money. Most ball games require two opposing players or teams for each competitive game traditionally. Why mostly only two? Pleasantly, the supreme beings think alike, but act on it, too.

To my amazement, I was given a chance to observe details on an eye-catching never-seen-before extraterrestrial ball game carefully attached to the enlightenment materials. Within an hour or so after the 2006 World Cup soccer final game ended, I was able to recall and jot down what I found. According to my two-page notes taken hastily at the time, I named it triball because three teams would play with a ball.

Although triball could be played in a triangular field since there were three separate teams to compete in a game, its arena appeared to be completely round in a circle with a radius of 35 yards in my estimation. The arena would yield as much real estate for a player as a rectangular soccer field. Unlike the soccer field, the arena had no straight lines but a circle and three equally-apart inner arcs of a 15-yard radius.

Holding the big circle with its both ends from inside, each arc hatched a circular sector with two arcs of different lengths, thereby constructing three identical circular sectors distributed equally apart within. In the centrum of the outer arc of a circular sector, a goal post arc with a 3-yard radius made of a single piece of 4-inch round metal pipe without a net stood vertically with its pipe ends buried six yards apart.

Now, going deeper into my observation notes taken from the enlightenment materials, I would like to show you their game of triball in earthly terms by detailing basic rules pertaining to its hardware, players, and software so to speak. Above all, its most crucial piece of hardware is a bouncing ball primarily designed for kicking by a foot wearing a shoe. A unique triball similar to a plain soccer ball is played with.

Revisiting the triball arena initially described above, I would like to assign a color code, i.e., blue, red or yellow, to each sector to visually distinguish three identical sectors for all people involved in playing, refereeing, watching, etc. As such, there are three goal post arcs with different colors to indicate respective sectors, i.e., blue sector, red sector or yellow sector. Other curves, dots or lines are colored white.

Quite uniquely, the arena shows off four white dots. One is called a center mark. It is located in the dead center of the circled arena. It designates a starting ball position at different times during a game or whenever a contest occurs. The other three dots are called a middle point. Each one is located on the outer circle itself. It conspicuously divides a partial arc between two adjacent circular sectors into halves.

At this time, I would like to assign a proper name to some arena parts to facilitate an understanding of the game. Each circular sector is called a blue sector, a red sector or a yellow sector. Colored goal post arcs are called a goal post. A sector is surrounded by an inner arc called a starting line and an outer arc called a goal line. A partial arc connecting a circular sector apex and a middle point is called a sideline.

As revealed before, all the supreme beings possess a unisex body regardless of a female or male soul. Therefore, they do maintain a triball team consisting of unisex players, but an equal number of female or male souls play in a team. It affords a fantastic idea to form a unisex human team, too, especially because it is a game of luck with strategy as well as skill. So men and women together could play or watch it.

As such, three different unisex teams play in a game. Each team deploys six players, i.e., five active players with an open position and a passive player with a goalie position. Additionally, at every moment in a game, each team has to maintain three men and three women regardless of position. A goalie shall be played by either a female or a male player. Also, each team has an unlimited right to substitute players.

Unlike football, triball should not be a contact sport primarily because men and women play together in a game. Thus its software, i.e., game rules, has captivating elements. Frankly, any form of aggressive action toward other players in an active use of body parts by bumping, grabbing, hitting, holding, hugging, kicking, pinching, striking, touching, etc. is banned. Sliding to a ball is okay if a ball contact is made.

Any active player committing a contact foul should remain grounded at the very spot until a team scores a goal. Such a player should not touch a ball while being penalized, or the player should stand inactive until two goals are made. Even so, the inactive player could be hit by a ball passively. A goalie, only passive player, is subject to the above rule as well. If the goalie violates, a goal post becomes wide-open.

Essentially, triball is played in three trimesters of 20 minutes each or 60 minutes in total with 10 minutes of rest period in between. If a list of game winners for each game, i.e., gold, silver, and bronze, is not determined at the end of the third trimester, extra extensions of 20 minutes each with 10 minutes of rest period in between are played until such a list is fully finalized at the end of each additional extension.

Basically, each and every goal is a scoring event for all three teams during a game. A team making a goal gets a score of 1, a team allowing a goal gets a score of -1, and the third party team gets a score of 0. A goal is scored if a ball goes into a goal post and falls outside a goal line somehow. In other words, a ball can also bounce off inside a goal line. A mechanical or electronic gadget is used to keep the score.

Aside from wearing a thick pair of protective gloves, a goal keeper or goalie should wear a uniform that is easily distinguishable from others in a team because he or she can catch, grasp, punch or throw a ball with hands unlike others. At any rate, a goalie cannot go out of a circular sector while a ball is live, i.e., being played in a big circle during a game. If such a rule is broken, a goalie gets substituted right away.

A goal scoring event is usually an exciting moment for any ball game. It is wise to allow easier goals in a game. In order to achieve such a lofty goal, triball is meticulously designed with four traits. First, a goal post has a maximum 3-yard vertical clearance which is a foot higher than soccer. Second, 6 players may struggle against 10 offensive players. Third, a goalie can be grounded. Fourth, a friend may help.

All the active players participate in either defensive or offensive moves without fixed positions depending upon situations or strategies. Anywhere within a big circle, they can use any part of their body except for their hands to play. If a live ball is touched by any part of hands either actively or passively, a hand foul is committed and the active player becomes inactive for grounding at the spot until a next goal.

Besides a contact foul against any players or a hand foul against a ball, there exist a quarrel foul and a start foul. When a dispute among players or against a referee becomes a quarrel often with a physical fight, a referee could issue a quarrel foul to everyone involved. If so, any spots could be chosen for grounding till a next goal. Also, for a false start, players could get a start foul for grounding until a next goal.

Just like soccer, if a ball goes through a goal line to land outside a big circle, the goalie can kick or throw a ball. A similarity with soccer ends there. Triball keeps a unique rule called a contest ball by either three teams or two teams. For a contest ball, a referee brings a ball to the center mark after all the active participating team players line up behind the starting line of their respective sectors and signals a run.

A contest by three happens at the beginning of each trimester or extension, right after a goal scoring event, after a quarrel foul is issued, and if a ball goes through a sideline while touching or passing above either a middle point or an apex of a circular sector. A contest by two takes place after a contact or hand foul and after a ball goes out of a sideline. Of course, a team with a guilty player can't participate in it.

Much like any other games, triball can be played in a league, a tournament or a combination of both including a wild card opportunity for any second and third spot winners. Since each game needs 3 teams, triball can be played by a 3 to the nth power number of teams, i.e., 3, 9, 27, 81 and 243, in a game progression such as a league, tournament or both. As such, 9 teams form each group to play at 3 game arenas.

A league system can be adopted for a regular season while a tournament system is suited for a final competition for 3 final teams, 9 semifinal teams or 27 quarterfinal teams. In each group of 9 teams, 3 games can be played to produce a list of respective gold, silver or bronze game winners first. Then, 3 more games are played to advance to the next level. Each game is played by gold, silver or bronze winners only.

As a result, only 3 gold winners from each game of the above fill the three spots for a final game within a group. In essence, the second and third spots are called a wild card because they are filled by a gold winner from a silver game and a gold winner from a bronze game. In the beginning of a season, 9 teams each are allocated to a group randomly or systematically. Game results must decide further groupings.

In order to minimize any chance of extra extensions, a team making the very first goal obtains the first advantage and a team making the very last goal gets the last advantage so that such a team can exercise its advantage in a tie score. Suddenly, I get kind of philosophical. The supreme beings showed triball to the human beings. Why? Any enemy can become a friend. From start to end, we all must do our best.

As I was given the enlightenment materials in 2006, I could have easily missed a whole boat pertaining to triball, but luckily I did not. Everything has a reason. So does this. Months before I happened to see the gigantic UFO in 1984, I visited KLA Instruments located here in Silicon Valley to review an R&D proposal designed to trigger a growth spurt. A plant tour made me excited for high technology business.

Based upon what I learned that day from one of the company founders, I was able to develop a new board game on my own time at home. It turned out to be a quite unique fun game based on luck, skill, and strategy. Albeit I did not know a thing at first about designing a playable board game from scratch, I could devise a standard process step by step. I even made a prototype of the intuitive easy-to-learn game.

In the process of developing and improving the new board game, I happened to gain an invaluable insight into a game area as to virtually all the ins and outs necessary for it. Surely, I must have acquired and maintained an aptitude or awareness towards other games like triball for instance. So, when the time came suddenly to pick up a brand-new game, I was fully ready to ingest the game. I didn't miss anything.

I have tested my board game for years. It takes only about 15 minutes on the average to play out a typical game. Also, I purposely designed it in a way that all its game rules would be extremely flexible to afford a maximum degree of creativity introduced and agreed on by all players involved. Incidentally I even applied an extraterrestrial concept of the third player to the game board in 2014, and it was a success.

TWENTY-ONE:
Two Tiny UFOs in My Eye

In one's life here on the earth, lots of things happen. Over time, certain things may formulate an obvious pattern. However, unless so many esoteric events keep cropping up, a genuinely dull or inert person hardly recognizes anything including a real meaning behind such a conspicuous design. I am talking about myself. Definitively, I am such a person. That is why it took me so long to unleash the whole picture. On the other hand, it may indicate that I am rather cautious. In fact, even after observing two more UFOs in an odd way, I still remained offstage quietly till a near-death experience.

My incredible sighting of the gigantic UFO back in 1984 proved to be just the first one of such in my life so far. Almost 24 years later, I did experience my second sighting. Unlike the first, I was not situated up-close this time around. I saw two UFOs at the same time, but I saw them indirectly. To be more precise, my second sighting was for two UFOs in the form of unique images embedded only in my left eye.

It was about 12:50 p.m. on February 10, 2008, to be exact. I was driving to the south on Bowers Avenue toward El Camino Real in Silicon Valley. At least several hundred yards prior to arriving at an intersection of those two streets, I suddenly started to murmur rather intensively with erratic screaming as well. Even my voice was a little bit trembling. I ended up blinking both eyes wildly, but I could still drive.

At the moment, I immediately felt that some foreign objects barged into my left eye even though I was of course wearing my glasses while driving my car with windows up. I could keep driving because my right eye was totally intact. The weather was clear. It was in fact sunny with no clouds whatsoever in the deep blue sky. The sun was right in front, but way up so high that I didn't even have a sun visor down.

In turn, it meant that I was not situated in a position to be bothered by any glare from the sun perhaps because it was directly above the car heading due south from the north. Further, I never got a shiny reflection of the sunlight, either. If there had been such, both eyes should have been affected. Although it happened so quickly, I sort of knew at once that an extremely strange phenomenon occurred out of nowhere.

Instantly, I was relying on an animalistic side of my instinct for a primary defensive mode against the unknown. Mainly because I could not promptly comprehend what was really happening to my left eye, I found myself panicking a little. As such, I couldn't even think about stopping the car. Thus, I kept talking out loud about a rather fearful situation which I was quickly up against while trying to figure it out.

Well, it had to happen when I was least expecting or prepared to see any extraterrestrial objects in the middle of driving with a business associate to a restaurant for a lunch meeting. All of a sudden, I had to deal with a set of distinct super-bright white images of two tiny spherical objects laid vertically spread in an angle of 60 degrees in my estimation. Oddly, I could detect or observe them with my left eye only.

To my surprise, the images were embedded at once onto the retinal center positioned in the back of my left eye as though a focused image was imprinted on a camera film. Interestingly, my retina was being used like a sheet of black & white negative film developed in less than a split second. As for the images that lasted at least for a couple of minutes, it took me about 30 seconds to realize that they were UFOs.

Except for tilting directions, they appeared identical in their spherical shape with their top dome disclosed to me. The bottom UFO was tilted up to the right as if flying to the right while the top UFO was tilted up to the left as if flying to the left. Beyond a reasonable doubt, a still frame for the two unidentified flying objects suggested clearly to me that it captured their well-choreographed zigzag departure mode.

Of course, I was already familiar with such a unique zigzag flight path flown by departing UFOs based upon my unforgettable up-close sighting of the gigantic UFO in 1984. Even though I was left with only a single screen shot of the moving objects in the air, I was able to recognize their cool zigzag flight path dashed by two UFOs flying in formation primarily due to their combined spread angle of 60 degrees.

Meantime, there existed yet another peculiar aspect thoroughly observed during a relatively long period of time while the retinal images remained exceptionally vivid to me. Each UFO had a circular wing dividing a sphere into halves. A top half comprised of a single perfect dome, but a bottom half with another dome presumably protruded upside down was not visible due to a one-sided positioning on the retina.

At any rate, each UFO exhibited a very conspicuous blackish gap along a horizontal curve on a spherical middle between a super-bright top dome and a super-bright circular wing as though both parts were never attached to each other. Also, all such sharp graphical images for the top dome and the circular wing didn't have any jagged edges around each. How was it possible? To this day, it has remained a puzzle.

Certainly, they were not produced by a reflection of the bright sunlight in any way. If they had been, the images should have shown jagged edges all around due to a natural characteristic of a retinal image associated with the sunlight. For instance, please stare at a super-bright light source for a while and close both of your eyes firmly. What do you see? You would never be able to find a cookie-cutter image of it.

Besides, such a rough super-bright reflective image would normally last shorter than a couple of minutes before completely disappearing from a retinal area of a human eye. However, the super-bright but neatly-sharpened images for the two tiny UFOs embedded on my retina lasted very long. In retrospect, it is terribly odd that my right eye or the other person in my car could not see any traces of the same UFOs.

Even after encountering the second and third UFOs in my life in the very center of the high-tech Silicon Valley, I was definitely too slow to recognize any significance with regard to a continual series of diverse extraterrestrial events, let alone any obvious pattern or its eventual hidden purpose. In hindsight, the supreme beings were aptly present behind each and every such experience beyond a reasonable doubt.

Just over two months later in April 2008, I abruptly found myself dealing with a so-called day of reckoning for the first time in my life. I was just driving back alone from Los Angeles, California, to Silicon Valley area in the north. On a somewhat safe mountainous stretch in the middle of a historically-dangerous freeway connecting major interstates, I got into a bad auto accident by myself due to carelessness.

Turning off Interstate 5 north, I was driving steadily on State 152 west so that I could get over to U.S. 101 north. I was about 10 miles into a 40-mile stretch of the State 152, enduring a rugged area with a vertical cliff standing by San Luis Reservoir on the farther left and a steep slope climbing a rocky mountain on the immediate right. Unknown to me, the shoulder was littered with fallen rocks broken to pieces.

For a sloppy reason, I made a sort of stupid mistake. I stepped onto the shoulder cluttered with all sizes of rocks. Because I was already doing a maximum speed of 65 MPH, I was destined to lose a control of my car on such a surface. As soon as I started hearing all the loose pieces of rocks hit the car bottom, the whole car began to shake quite violently. No matter how hard I put on the brake, the car kept moving.

Oddly enough, from the very moment of getting off a freeway lane by mistake, I could not see anything in front although I kept my eyes wide-open. Soon, I could not hear anything and everything although I kept my ears wide-open. During all the above, I knew that I was still fully conscious. Physiologically speaking, I was experiencing a weird stage of sensory deprivation with regard to my own eyes and ears.

Of course, I could have been wrong to a degree, but I never lost consciousness yet during such a shocking stage. I certainly remember that I was totally comfortable or even emotionally warm without a single fear at the time because I felt like going through a densely-fogged gray-lighted area under absolute quietness or complete silence. I was certain I was dying. Time slowed down. I reviewed my entire life.

Even then, I still had more time left over until death. It was strange that I was actually approaching my final gate, but I wasn't fearful at all. Instead, I was eager to end a life. In fact, I was asking me when the whole process would end. As I recall now, I did not go through a narrow tunnel with a bright light at the end. I saw nobody who had passed away. Yet, it was so obvious that I was getting very close to death.

Finally in the end, I was taken entirely out of myself at least for a while. Not long after the awful accident ended, I gradually found myself dangling upside down inside a car. It was my own car, but I certainly did not have all the detail except that I got into an automobile accident on the freeway. I began to think briskly for survival since I smelt a burning. I needed to escape my flipped car before being hit by others.

It was another poor mistake on my part, but I hastily pressed a bright red button to release a seat belt without any way of supporting my own weight being dropped head first. I heard a surprising cracking sound coming out of my chest, but I kind of ignored it. I could kick open a door to get out. Once out of the car rolled over to the middle of the freeway, I didn't even know why, but I was walking all over the spot.

Soon, quite a few caring people stopped and got out of their cars to help me out at the accident scene. About ten Caucasian men and women were gathered there to carry out respective tasks such as calling 911, picking up debris from the freeway, directing the traffic in the middle of mountains, advising me to stay put since I could be injured, looking for my lost cell phone, etc. till the emergency vehicles came by.

As I was warned in advance by a young army medic who was on a short leave from the Iraq War, I finally found myself very difficult to breathe when an ambulance arrived. A nearby hospital emergency was more than 30 miles away through a mountainous area. Being strapped onto a gurney, I gave each and every kind person who remained to the end a big hug. I really felt joung, i.e., a genuine human warmth.

Inside the moving ambulance, a paramedic checked my vital signs. I opened my eyes. He asked me how many fingers he was waving at me. As I replied to him correctly, he threw at me something utterly significant out of the blue. With a warm smile, he said, "Welcome to your second life!" According to him, there was a huge black skid mark on the side of the freeway going up on the slope to roll down from.

Cherishing his welcome message on my second life, I pondered upon what to do with my extra time on the earth. I wanted to do something really meaningful, but I could not figure out readily what it should be. In a couple of months, I decided to unravel my exciting extraterrestrial experience. For three years, among others, I wrote nine short essays on UFO sightings, enlightenment, etc. Then I stopped writing.

The ninth essay was completed on January 16, 2011. Since all such astounding essays were composed in Korean for a small group of curious online readers mostly in Korea, an overall impact on the earth population was very minimal. Besides, I did not write anything further with regard to any extraterrestrial subject for nearly four long years afterwards. As such, the supreme beings could have disappointed in me.

However, I could never find a serious motivation on my part for unleashing what I was able to accumulate so far in terms of anything and everything related to the whole big picture based upon the universal life system operation rules. As a result, the whole subject was on the back burner in my mind virtually forever until March 8, 2014, when one of the most mysterious incidents in human history began to unfold.

TWENTY-TWO:
Whereabouts of MH370 (1)

Most people refer to the missing MH370 plane case as a mystery in aviation, but it appears to be more than that. As corroborated in detail by the whole content in this book, the case should be classified as a mystery in human history. A logical approach in the next two chapters pays off nicely in an attempt to solve the puzzling mystery once and for all. It is amazing to see that most all of the mysterious elements seem to be melting away clean when a critical technique of thinking outside the box is applied to this case. At any rate, this analysis points to a direction of extraterrestrial reason.

When worldwide breaking news about the Malaysia Airlines flight MH370 was broadcasted, I did not even pay close attention to it. An airplane would suddenly disappear from any radar screen and briskly reappear in any condition, either good or bad, in any part of our world at any moment. It was sad for all the precious people unaccounted for, but it was frankly another piece of news to me on March 8, 2014.

Well, it had remained as such in my mind only until I happened to see network TV news on a revised flight path allegedly picked up by the Malaysian military radar system. As soon as I saw the crazy flight path on the TV screen that clearly showed a quick left turn at an unusually sharp angle going due west off the original route from Kuala Lumpur in Malaysia to Beijing in China, my mood changed in a hurry.

From the outset, it was quite apparent with regard to what was missing, when it happened, and where it vanished. Accordingly, the very first international search efforts took place in the South China Sea. Within days, the search area was expanded to the Gulf of Thailand, the Strait of Malacca, and the Andaman Sea based on new, shocking, strange, and weird information. However, not a single trace was spotted.

As such, the whole missing case quickly grew up to be branded as one of the most puzzling mysteries in history. Basically, virtually all the human beings on the earth asked four annoying or baffling questions. Who did it? Why did they do it? How did they do it? Where is the missing plane? All of the comprehensive, meticulous, and tenacious search works in the southern Indian Ocean has produced no results.

Equipped with my extraterrestrial insight, subjective instinct, objective intuition, cumulative knowledge, rational logic, and accurate interpretation from complete analysis of all those critical pertinent facts regarding the flight MH370, I would attempt to unravel the complex mystery in terms of who, why, and how to the best of my capability. So please help me, the supreme beings. In essence, they are still alive.

Frantically, there have been all kinds of possibilities expressed in theories imagined or produced by people from all different walks of life virtually everywhere on the globe with regard to dismantling the mystery as to who, why, and how, but none has come up with a convincing whereabouts. It may sound crazy to those people who aren't aware of the whole big picture, but it can be solved using unearthly facts.

As a matter of fact, it should make a perfect sense to those people who became aware of the whole big picture on how the universal life system should operate in the universe and the fact that the earth should prove to be one of the soul farms created, managed, and visited by the supreme beings. As for me, upon learning of the flight path with a sharp turn, I could afford an immediate visualization of what happened.

At that point in time, I only sensed that the supreme beings must have done it so as to start or strengthen another ready-made soul farm on a planet not too far from the earth. Except for who and why, I was still clueless on exactly how. Frankly, the job pulled off by the supreme beings in charge of such a task might appear genuinely shocking to our eyes. However, it could have been a routine job to them in reality.

The above revelation should explain who did it and why they did it, but logical, plausible, and scientific details on exactly how they did it would not be materialized easily. As for the very question of how, a persuasive set of detailed answers would rise in my mind only after being bombarded with so much critical information uncovered or volunteered and weird incidents seemingly unrelated but directly related.

Based on my extraterrestrial viewpoint accumulated, corroborated, focused, and sharpened for way over 30 years, all 227 passengers and 12 crew members from 15 countries aboard the Malaysian flight MH370 have been relocated to another soul farm by the supreme beings so that they could augment an existing civilization or initiate a brand-new one on a planet similar to the earth. As such, they are still alive.

Just like everyone else, I am an earthly human being. I am fully capable of making mistakes including one on this. Even so, my own out-of-the-box disposition of the missing airplane case presented above has satisfied all my curiosity as well as intelligence beyond reasonable doubt in my mind. As such, to me, it's not only a theory or truth but also a fact. Otherwise, how could anyone explain the unsolved mystery?

Besides certain confirmed wing parts like a flaperon, no other Boeing 777 parts found so far in the Indian Ocean peripheries have been directly linked to the missing aircraft. Just think about how fast most other plane wreckages have been found by so many concerned people around the globe. For instance, wreckages for the German Airbus and another Malaysian flight MH17 were located in hours, respectively.

Of course, the above two planes crashed to the land, the former into the French Alps on March 24, 2015, and the latter which was another Boeing 777 in Ukraine on July 17, 2014, thus easier to be located. However, crashing into the sea should make practically not much difference in terms of easiness in locating, for virtually all the airplanes would be totally disintegrated into pieces upon impact on the surface.

Further, especially all the hundreds of seat cushions would be automatically separated from each and every seat and float forever in the sea according to experts in the field. Assuming that the missing flight crashed not to the land but to the sea, it does not make any sense that not even a single piece of the seat cushions from the plane has been found in the sea or washed up on a beach in any place for that matter.

Certainly, like the unpowered emergency landing of the US Airways flight 1549 on the Hudson River pulled off aptly by Captain Chesley Sullenberger on January 15, 2009, Captain Zaharie Ahmad Shah might have lowered the flight MH370 with a controlled ditching technique somewhere in the southern Indian Ocean and sunken to the bottom slowly. Despite of the search, there has not been a single trace there.

Besides, it is highly unlikely that any human beings onboard the flight including the captain himself could have maintained consciousness or recovered it fully a while later after being fainted quickly by erratic flight maneuvers with incredibly steep ups and downs into totally crazy directions in acute angles as soon as it suddenly disappeared from the air traffic control radar screens in Malaysia and in Vietnam.

One day certainly in the last ten days of March 2014, I happened to listen to an overnight radio talk show intently on either AM 810 KGO or AM 910 KKSF via iHeartRadio on my laptop while working in my office till after midnight. A male host invited a female engineer on the phone and the two engaged in a critical conversation on the missing flight MH370 very intensively for a relatively long period of time.

Based upon my recollection, she mentioned that the aircraft engines for all the Boeing 777 planes were made by Rolls-Royce, that all the jet engines were equipped with an independent transmission device for an hourly ping directly sent to Rolls-Royce, and that each ping would be an e-mail filled with all sorts of consecutive hourly performance data for each engine whether or not being operated in any places.

In an assertive, concise, methodical, and quiet voice, she continued to mention that her job at Rolls-Royce was to collect all such engine data pings received from all over the globe and analyze them in detail. According to her remarks, she had never seen throughout her professional career such a weird set of engine data collected from the flight MH370 regularly for some hours even after its initial disappearance.

Based upon her complete analysis of the engine data, the missing plane apparently made erratic flight maneuvers which were totally out of whack for any Boeing 777 planes. She was shocked to realize that the flight MH370 ascended 13,000 feet in only a minute from 32,000 feet to 45,000 feet and then descended 23,000 feet in only a minute from there to 22,000 feet right after its disappearance for the first time.

Their serious conversation went on further to reveal that a Boeing 777 airplane wasn't designed in the first place to climb all the way up to 45,000 feet, that it was definitely impossible to ascend 13,000 feet or descend 23,000 feet all within one minute respectively, and that no one could have used an oxygen mask due to an overwhelming shock factor although it should've dropped automatically on the way up.

Toward the end of their conversation, the host asked the engineer what should have happened to all those people on the plane during such a drastic ascending or descending. Without hesitation, she replied that everybody including the cockpit crew could have been still conscious on the way up, but should have completely fainted or become unconscious on the way down. It must've been far worse than a free fall.

Indisputably, neither the host nor the engineer could even understand how the whole thing got unfolded as it did. With candor, they seemed to be fully convinced that it was absolutely quite a mystery especially after exchanging their own genuine perspectives with incredibly shocking content. However, I was quietly thinking fast pursuing my own line of thought pertaining to the supreme beings and soul farms.

Frankly speaking, even at that point, I didn't have a clear connection or picture of exactly how the huge Boeing 777 aircraft was captured to be jerked around like a rag doll in such an acute flight path with a set of steep up and down. Before completing her revealing conversation with the host, she added that there were actually numerous sets of drastic ups and downs, departing from the known information then.

Lo and behold, the Malaysian military officials soon admitted rather reluctantly that their military radar tracking systems detected its westerly flight path pretty sporadically whenever it barged into a certain altitude range of air space. A conspicuous absence of their remarks on a puzzled flight path of the airplane with drastic ups and downs in actuality revealed that nobody could explain the whole thing exactly.

On March 31, 2014, CNN reported very briefly that a group of young Chinese engineers volunteered from some families, friends, and relatives staying in a big Beijing hotel had completed an in-depth analysis project with all sorts of critical flight data details from diverse information sources and meticulously rendered a detailed flight path on how the missing flight actually made such an acute or sharp left turn.

According to what I saw clearly on the CNN report, they concluded after their own research analysis efforts that the missing plane should have actually made two clockwise circles or loops with a considerable length in diameter each instead of a single sharp left turn as suggested in the visual flight path previously announced by the Malaysian officials. With no further ado, they made a perfect sense in the report.

However, they explained a little further, standing in front of the rectangular presentation white board which had their own version of the manually-drawn flight path in blue ink as I recall, that they only assumed two smoothly-circled flight loops considering a limited maneuverability of a huge Boeing 777 airplane although the actual flight data analysis suggested quite a few unimaginable movements. Oh, yeah!

TWENTY-THREE:
Whereabouts of MH370 (2)

On April 2, 2014, I happened to spot a horoscope of Leo for the day before from Susan Miller's Astrology Zone. She posted, "You may receive a flash of insight that upends your understanding (of the mystery) or a spark that leads to new (revealing) truths. Don't be afraid to shake things up." Of course, it should have been a simple case of coincidence, but I felt quite a bit strange or weird right after digesting it because of what actually happened to me on the day before. I did really receive a sudden flash of incredible insight that effectively contributed to solving the flight MH370 mystery.

Normally, I would seldom wake up in the middle of sleep at night and in fact get up on my own to do something. However, I did just that on April 1, 2014, i.e., the day after the CNN report on the newly-asserted flight path was aired. Slightly before 4:49 a.m., I did wake up all of a sudden due to a telepathic message pertaining to how to solve the flight MH370 mystery. For sure, it was from somebody up there.

Immediately, I got up and grabbed whatever I could in order to put down in writing a core concept of the insight. According to two pieces of notes with several drawings and a single graph, which I finished rather quickly by 5:15 a.m., its super-bright idea was to replace or substitute the looped flight path declared by the sharp-minded Chinese engineers with a unique zigzag flight path of the UFO that did the job.

Upon successfully completing the surprisingly short notes explaining the out-of-the-box core concept expressed in a compact but comprehensive manner, I was mesmerized by its ingenuity. Even its intricate format looked ingenious. In essence, the two circles or loops on the elaborated flight path were to be replaced or substituted with two equivalent triangles positioned properly in the middle of the flight path.

Instead of making one acute or sharp left turn, while flying in the northeast direction from Kuala Lumpur toward Beijing, the missing airplane was presumed by the Chinese engineers as having to make two separate circles or loops in order to switch its direction to the west due to its limitation. However, according to the extraterrestrial insight, the plane did not have to go through circles or loops for an acute turn.

Instead, from a fixed aerial viewpoint directly above the incident scene situated in the South China Sea between Malaysia and Vietnam, the Boeing 777-200ER aircraft with 2 Rolls-Royce engines for Malaysia Airlines flight MH370 took off from Kuala Lumpur International Airport at 00:41, confirmed the cruising altitude of 35,000 feet at 01:01, and finished its very last voice contact with the ground at 01:19.

Several minutes later at 01:22, the airplane vanished from the air traffic control radars in Malaysia and Vietnam because its transponder was suddenly disabled or turned off because its primary electrical power was completely cut off because its aircraft engines all of a sudden stopped working because a gigantic UFO swiftly captured the whole airplane and disabled everything instantly while dropping 3,000 feet.

Several minutes later at 01:25, the aircraft was fully secured to the UFO by being attached solidly at the bottom and started to go through a wacky flight path with the UFO. In reality, it was on a zigzag flight path steered by the UFO. Obviously, the airplane was not placed or stored in its body. If it had been, even the Malaysian military radars could not have picked it up sporadically here and there up until 02:22.

Over the first five minutes between 01:25 and 01:30, the UFO took the plane on the unique zigzag flight path by going up 13,000 feet from 32,000 feet to 45,000 feet in one minute, going down 23,000 feet from 45,000 feet to 22,000 feet in one minute, and so forth for five ups or downs in all while switching its direction from the northeast to the west. Those five straight lines form the two triangles from above.

In fact, in order to corroborate graphically the above crazy or wacky zigzag flight path, the graph was composed in terms of altitude from 0 feet to 45,000 feet or higher and time from 00:41 to 02:22 while emphasizing 01:25 to 01:30. Such a flight path could never be readily understood by any of us humans with lack of extraterrestrial knowledge yet on the whole big picture of the universal life system operation.

Frankly, although I wrote the notes myself with the graph and drawings according to the extraterrestrial insight, it wasn't even easy for me to visualize the actual flight path. On April 1, 2014, I went to work in the morning with a coat hanger and a pair of pliers in my briefcase. After finishing lunch quickly, I cut a wire off the coat hanger, straightened it, and bent it in angles to come up with a flight path model.

It was a success. As expected, it worked beautifully. By looking at the wire model of the zigzag flight path from a certain angle or viewpoint while holding it up in my hand, I could clearly observe the two triangles going up and down. They presented the same triangles as the ones shown on the notes. In its own way, the weird-looking wire model would visually confirm what the Rolls-Royce engineer mentioned.

In the meanwhile, the missing aircraft could emit or transmit several different types of mechanical or electronic pings to outside at certain intervals to be detected in case of emergency or to be monitored on its general well-being and specific maintenance scheduling needs. First, its two black boxes, i.e., a cockpit voice recorder in the front and a flight data recorder in the rear, could generate a ping as being wet.

Second, as discussed in the previous chapter, its two aircraft engines could generate an hourly electronic ping to transmit over to Rolls-Royce directly and independently as well while reporting all sorts of performance data measured in each hour, including altitude and time data among others. Unfortunately, I picked up no intricate details on how such a setup worked exactly except that each ping was an e-mail.

Third, as known, a computer system on board could emit, generate, send or transmit an hourly electronic ping to designated satellites so as to exchange an hourly handshake. One of the British satellites, Inmarsat-3F1, above the Indian Ocean was involved in the case of the subject flight MH370. This ping seems to be totally different from the second ping reiterated above, for it does not contain altitude information.

If you want to make a real impact on a tough matter, you could go to extremes so as to breed a lightning solution once and for all. You could look at all the options available either in the box or out of the box. The latter could be most effective according to my own brainstorming efforts in life. To me, the missing flight MH370 case wasn't an exception. It turned out that the whole incident occurred out of the box.

According to the Malaysian military radar detection at 02:22, the missing plane's last confirmed position was at 230 miles northwest of Penang, Malaysia. If so, it reached there in the southern Andaman Sea to the west of the Strait of Malacca while being handled around by the UFO exactly for an hour since 01:22 when it was taken in one scoop and got paralyzed electrically, electronically, and mechanically.

From the last known aerial position at 02:22, where did the missing aircraft for the Malaysian flight MH370 go? Early on and even up until now, all the experts and officials have concentrated their grueling international search efforts in multiple target areas of the southern Indian Ocean off the coast of Australia after choosing the southern route over the northern route based on a scientific study of ping frequency.

Apparently, they must have never even considered a possibility of another crucial route toward a different planet. As far as I could determine from my extraterrestrial insight, if and only if the upward route were adopted in the missing plane's case, virtually all the mysterious elements found in so many strange or weird flight details would make sense to all open-minded earthly human beings with common sense.

Interestingly, one of the most peculiar aspects to me of the third ping briefly explained above was its automation. Whenever the power was on, the onboard computer system did generate an electronic ping towards the Inmarsat-3F1 in accordance with a programmed set of the designated hourly time schedule in order to exchange an automatic handshake. It even sent a partial ping at 02:25 when power was back on.

At 00:41, it took off. At 01:01, it was at 35,000 feet. At 01:19, it finished the last voice contact. At 01:22, it was captured, incapacitated, and disappeared from the air traffic control radars. At 01:25, it began the zigzag flight with the UFO at 32,000 feet. Everyone was knocked out on purpose. At 01:30, it began to prepare for an interplanetary travel by dumping its jet fuel, etc. At 02:22, it began the space travel.

At 01:07, it sent an hourly ping. At 02:03, it missed a ping due to blackout. At 02:25, it sent a partial ping with a log-on request since the UFO restored power for a reason. It was already far above the Malaysian military radar range. At 03:41, it resumed to transmit a ping regularly. At 08:11, it fired off the sixth regular hourly ping. At 08:19, it sent a partial ping with a log-on request due to power interruption.

Since its disappearance, the missing aircraft sent six complete pings and two partial pings in total to the satellite. It meant that the aircraft was going up on the upward route for about 6.87 hours at the most from 02:22 to 09:14 before it missed all of the hourly pings scheduled at or after 09:15. What would this actually mean after all? Well, it should be a crucial extraterrestrial clue to prove what really happened.

At the time, the Inmarsat-3F1 was stationed directly above the equator at an altitude of about 22,400 miles and a longitude of 64.5 degrees in the middle of the Indian Ocean. The missing incident theater with the last detected position of the plane was located in the farthest eastern corner of the Indian Ocean from the viewpoint of the satellite on its duty, which was to detect earthly signals including all such pings.

Meanwhile, as elaborated earlier, a full-blown speed of the UFO which brought my just-passed-away aunt to me flying over the vast Pacific Ocean in 2 hours was calculated to be factually 3,000 miles per hour. Under the same speed flown, the airplane must have reached an altitude of 20,600 miles in 6.87 hours, which was perhaps a peripheral ceiling from an umbrella effect of the earthly signal detection field.

Effectively, it explains why the Inmarsat-3F1 hasn't picked up a single ping from the missing aircraft since then. In addition, there was an astounding incident in April 2014. A 15-year-old stowaway survived a five-hour trip from San Jose to Maui inside a Boeing 767's landing gear wheel well. Flying across the Pacific Ocean at an altitude of 38,000 feet, he endured both oxygen depletion and subzero temperature.

According to him, he jumped over the runway fence, climbed to the well, fell asleep, but woke up during takeoff. However, he was swiftly knocked out while ascending and regained his consciousness slowly an hour after touchdown. According to medical experts, he hardly needed oxygen air due to heart inactivity because he instantly got frozen alive. The UFO adopted the same technique for the flight MH370.

Based on my close observation of the gigantic UFO back in 1984, which looked surprisingly fragile to my eyes, the whole body of the missing Boeing 777 should be sturdy enough to withstand any type of interplanetary space travel including slipping through wormholes. The New Horizons spacecraft for instance looks too fragile, but it flew about 3 billion miles to pass by Pluto on July 14, 2015, in 9.5 years.

Now, in terms of exposing or revealing whereabouts of the missing Malaysia Airlines flight MH370 in this book, everything has been said and done as far as I am concerned. Totally or partially, I could be either right or wrong about it, but I just wanted to convey what I sort of knew almost from the outset of the tremendous incident. In fact, I was finally motivated to write this book to say this: They are still alive.

TWENTY-FOUR:
I Witnessed Another UFO

This finishes the whole big picture and dawnvolism hit by the Books of Changes, Rights, Eastern Scriptures, etc. My actual march to this book began back in 1984. Even so, I was reckless indeed to start writing on November 6, 2014, holding only a few materials in hand. Yet, humming Frank Sinatra's 'My Way' tune, I stepped into uncharted universe. I got shocked to realize the presence of the supreme beings. For all practical purposes, they wrote and edited this book. They designed, planned, reviewed, and supervised it as well. In spite of refusal, I also listed them as authors to be honest.

Two weeks into this odd project, I was still working on the very first chapter. Truly, I was struggling quite a bit, for I was not used to writing a book from scratch especially in English. Luckily, to my satisfaction, I was able to decide on a page format from one of my favorite books titled 'The Measure of a Man' written by Sidney Poitier that one of my daughters gave me as a thoughtful birthday present in 2008.

Shortly after midnight on November 21, 2014, I was on my way home upon finalizing the last sentence firmly in my draft copy of the first chapter on upshot of truth vs. fact. It was a question: What is the purpose of our existence here? So soon after externalizing the question, I saw another UFO. Was it a coincidence? No, it was not. I never knew it then, but I was to catch a visual answer from the supreme beings.

I realized it only in hindsight on July 16, 2015, wow! It was their awesome, ingenious, meticulous, and profound plan for me to view yet another extraterrestrial flying object. On July 15, 2015, I casually scraped a dried food-like stick off an old page of my draft. Next day, I realized that it was a 5/8-inch-long visual marker pointing at the very question. Was it a worm on a telepathic action order to slip in and die?

What could be an answer to the question on purpose? By now, anyone who has paid attention to this book should come up with the one and only correct answer comfortably. According to the whole big picture about how the universal life system works, the most important purpose of existence for the human beings on the earth soul farm is to cultivate a soul to be more mature in a lifetime for the supreme beings.

If and only if everything works out okay as planned, a blank or empty soul goes through an incarnation followed by multiple reincarnations into human bodies one at a time to become fully mature as quickly as possible so that it can be harvested and taken to a distant planet to lead an eternal life in a supreme body along with the other supreme beings. As you can see clearly, the whole system is notably simple.

If you sit down serenely and think about it seriously, a real beauty of the whole system lies with a clever fact that virtually nobody knows until after death whether their soul is fully mature or not. So everyone has to do the best in life. Even so, certain people may know or sense that their soul is fully mature and that their soul will leave the earth for good. Jesus Christ served a good example of it as elaborated later.

Now, I would like to explain what I happened to see in the midst of Silicon Valley while driving home alone just a little after the midnight on November 21, 2014. I was on the Freeway 280 southbound heading towards east actually. Soon I switched onto the Freeway 87 southbound making a broad right turn on the oddly-designed freeway interchange. The ground was deeply soaked wet by earlier frequent rains.

As such, the entire night sky looked especially crisp due to even the lightly-polluted air being cleaned out by all the raindrops. I saw distinct small puffy clouds littered low. As I was coming up from the right turn to drive to the south, I soon suddenly noticed vaguely at first but succinctly later that there was a big bright light in the distance a little to the left of the Freeway 87. I focused on the area as I got closer.

In effect, I was only playing a curious rubbernecker. I was in fact expecting to pass by and observe an overnight construction site with super-bright floodlights over the area to work on a tall building or something, but I realized soon in a hurry as I was getting closer to it that I was dead wrong. I quickly pulled myself together. Hence, even though I was doing 65 MPH, I did grasp the whole scene in quite a detail.

Within about 30 seconds in total of dealing with the brightly-lit area from start to end, the first 15 seconds or so were kind of wasted since I did not think much of it mainly due to a distance issue. However, the last 15 seconds or so were entirely different. My animalistic instinct took charge of my eyes with glasses on so that I could see to remember anything and everything filling the whole mysterious scene.

Just like my abrupt observation of the gigantic UFO in 1984, I had absolutely no time to analyze what the whole thing was all about. Instead, my eyes worked fast capturing basic factual elements. Such a condensed mind-set allowed me to stretch each precious second to the longest amazingly. Except only for my eyes, I felt like I was actually appearing in a slow-motion picture, giving ample time for observation.

What I could witness in haste with awe through the front windshield and the driver side door window of my car was a massive round flat disk object engaged in an activity. It looked as if it was sitting on an edge of a rectangular tall building constructed perpendicular to the freeway next to it. Actually, it was floating in the air right next to the building at an altitude of about 10 feet higher than the top of the roof.

Apparently, its diameter was quite impressive to me since it appeared as long as or even slightly longer than the width of the big building itself. It was floating in a slanted way so that I could observe its round flat bottom, not its top. Though it was in an operational mode, there was absolutely no mechanical noise being generated. It was quiet or silent. Sharply, I saw three super-bright light beams coming down.

Obviously, each light beam was neither a floodlight nor a typical searchlight because it was not being dispersed but being focused while descending from a big light source. In fact, the round flat disk was constantly wobbling slightly as if it was trying to focus its three light beams into a space through a chosen window on a freeway side of the building. My instinct alerted me that it was doing a sophisticated task.

Speaking of the light source, the whole disk bottom looked like a huge tray holding four big dishes of equal size. All such dishes represented a respective lamp for red, green, blue or yellow light. With a conspicuous exception for the fourth lamp at the far right of the disk bottom, all the lamps were illuminating a respective red, green or blue light beam. As such, I saw largely a natural combination of those lights.

From a dynamic vantage point while on the freeway, I could see both the top and the bottom of all light beams in different angles, the former in a separate color and the latter in a combined color for super-bright white light. Since the built-in color lamps were located very close to each other, a separate color could be visible only around each lamp itself. The yellow lamp with grid was on, but it had no light beam.

The whole scene was extremely strange, weird, and even scary a little because I had never seen anything like it. Indeed, I had no idea whatsoever as to what it was all about. Only after passing the last vantage point, I was able to think of stopping the car on the side in order to take some photos. However, I actually hesitated since there were no other cars on the freeway. Soon it became too late for me to pull over.

During the day, I was not even sure what I observed. I never thought I saw a UFO mainly because I was not able to see a dome either at the bottom or at the top of the object and partly because I felt that it kind of looked like a Disney animation in a way perhaps due to super-bright light beams. However, an in-depth talk with a friend in video equipment business made me realize quickly that it was a unique UFO.

The next day, I took a close look at all the elements involved including all the surroundings in the area by using Google Maps and by driving through the same stretch again. It turned out that it was the only tall building in the vicinity, that it looked like a ten-story condominium with a width of 100 feet and a length of 200 feet, and that it stood less than 100 yards from the closest moving vantage point at the time.

Moreover, the above points clearly suggested to me that the round flat disk had a diameter of over 100 feet, that each round flat lamp certainly had a diameter of at least 30 feet, that a separate area to house a command control center was most likely on the other side of the round flat disk, and that it must have been a UFO per all the above conclusions. Finally, it dawned on me that it was projecting a 3-D figure.

As exposed in the earlier chapter on a mature soul's journey, the supreme beings would carry out such a special task projecting a life-sized 3-D figure or hologram in color for a fully mature soul harvested if an appeal to visit people of choice could turn out to be logistically feasible based on pertinent facts and circumstances. After an event, it would be taken away forever from the earth to have an eternal life.

For instance, it was the case with my late aunt when I suddenly encountered her standing next to my bed at night on November 24, 2004. Although I was quite curious as to how it was actually conducted, I had no way of figuring out. For a reason, the supreme beings must've decided to let me see the whole projection scene as an answer to my question on the purpose of our existence. We are to get fully mature.

In the case of Jesus Christ, he certainly knew not all but enough details about the whole big picture based on his enlightenment materials conveyed from the supreme beings. Hence, he sensed in advance that his soul was fully mature, that he would be taken away, and even that he could appeal to return for a brief visit to see his followers upon his death. Accordingly, he could and did predict his own resurrection.

Apparently, his brave, faithful, intelligent, and wise stunt played out pretty well as planned by him methodically. The supreme beings had no objections to his proposed plan subject to workable logistics. So they enacted sophisticated capacious gigs of 3-D figure or hologram projection service in front of his followers in different areas for multiple days. Afterwards, his soul was taken forever, never to be returned.

To sum up the book and to start up a logical religion, the supreme beings dispatched me two dreams and subdued a nightmare for me on July 5, 2015. Later on July 12, 2015, they issued me a dream on my competency. Details follow: First, 21 people exited the office restroom on my assurance. Inside, I found a lady with a girl at a backdoor just arriving and a chef sitting high on an elevated toilet in a glass room.

They were 24 squatters. As such, I decided to settle with 24 chapters, i.e., 21 finished, two planned for analysis of the MH370, and one vacated for a sort of religious finale. Second, the same dream continued after an hour. I returned home for dinner to find people cold and hungry in our yard. We only had rice with potatoes for three, but we let them in. A couch did not fit all. Most sat on the floor to eat and talk.

Our food for 3 fed 27. Some brushed teeth and took a shower. I realized that they were the same 24 Caucasians. I asked a blonde girl on the couch whether they were a cult. Her eyes were erased, meaning a negative. Third, all kinds of colorful devils one by one attacked me savagely. I woke up each time in horror. I had not dreamed such a nightmare. At last, I had to ask the supreme beings for help. It worked.

Fourth, I ate a golden apple at a stand in a grey city. People there yelled that I was to die since it was poisonous. A paramedic came to stick a huge syringe into my left thigh to sample. He cleared me safe with a mobile lab test report and read it out loud, "You are fully capable and qualified to help others for a small fee." However, I have no interest in religion, for I'm not religious. I'd like to just enlighten you.

Epilogue

Other than a handful of written notes, I had no plans, but I knew up front that this book would garner 28 chapters. I consecutively drafted the first 21 chapters, but I could not write a single word for the next 4 chapters albeit I had tried so hard for a week. Later, I sensed that the supreme beings in charge of the project changed their mind and decided not to comingle fiction and nonfiction stories in the same book.

In fact, those 4 chapters would have been dedicated to synopsizing a fun movie regarding the whole big picture as an entertainment on how the universal life system works. Amazingly, the movie clip was attached to the enlightening telepathic mail sent to me from the supreme beings in 2006. Apparently, they were even agonized over how to introduce the shocking brand-new core concepts in a friendly fashion.

Appraising a persuasion quality of work in progress, they must have felt confident that nonfiction material alone could open up our new world for all walks of human beings. As if to convince me, they even sent me a telepathic dream featuring 24 squatters assembled. Therefore, it was natural for me to wrap up this fascinating extraterrestrial book with only 24 nonfiction chapters in order to rescue our humanity.

Throughout the whole duration of this book project, the supreme beings helped me out a great deal in real terms. Besides working with me very diligently on the manuscript, they in fact selected the first page design out of four created. They even recommended 'Soul Farm' as a book title. Thus, I used mine 'The Purpose of UFOs & Humans' as a subtitle. These revelations may sound weird, but they are all factual.

They are not perfect much like us the human beings. Aside from their intention to let us cultivate judgment skills utilizing free will, this book discusses many different issues, but it shows a conspicuous absence on many difficult issues like drug abuse among others. What is wrong with relying on recreational drugs when more and more American states are changing their laws to allow some cannabis for instance?

The most important purpose of our life on the earth soul farm is to make our soul fully mature for a planned use. For such a lofty goal, we should do our best to keep its case, i.e., our brain, as healthy as possible while keeping it intact. We'd better even do away with any gateway drugs that can eventually lead to terminal addiction of hallucination drugs, for we have limitless alternatives to boost our brain happier.

In order to achieve the above successfully in a cinch, everybody dealing with such a precarious personal situation should ask oneself a crucial but simple question employing all the necessary tools picked up from this fascinating book: Is it good for maturing my soul while not harming my body? Our life with body and soul is not really ours to waste at all. Of course, you have a complete freedom to believe it or not.

There was a boy. He did not take a bus after school for months to save money to land a set of used GED books. He gave it to a poor boy near school, surprising him with a chance of education. In 1973, a wise friend made him toss two coins to pick one hexagram sign out of 64 illustrated in 'The Book of Changes' - an ancient Far East divination text. Strikingly, he pulled the only revolution sign twice in a row.

The boy spent a year in college studying philosophy. He warily followed his aunt and sat down away from a lady. He observed in silence a fortune-telling. She eyeballed him. She told her that he would cross a huge body of water soon. Literally, he soon did cross such water to arrive in America. He began his new life as a busboy in a big Italian restaurant. Looking for a better job, he walked into an army boot camp.

A drill sergeant handled him like a deaf Gomer Pyle. He accepted it. Not knowing the language was his problem. One hot day, his platoon faced a towering triangular ladder with horizontal steps six feet apart. There was no safety net. Nobody volunteered since it was too dangerous to climb up. So hauntingly, he raised his hand in the rear for a challenge. He was the first to try. At its very top, he turned into a man.

Earning an honorable discharge from the U.S. Army, he restarted college on a GI Bill for business administration. Soon after, he began his career as a defense contract auditor. He could only draft audit reports which were clumsy at best. Graciously, he was under a thoughtful audit supervisor who took time and effort to lead him right into a special training on effective writing skills. He ended up learning quite a bit.

Throughout his short life here on the earth soul farm, he was assisted by many guardian angels like everyone else. Among them, there were two acupuncturists with rare skills. In 1986, he was diagnosed with an incurable kidney disease leaking a fair amount of protein and red blood cells in urine. He was gravely devastated, but quickly led to a mysterious Chinese acupuncturist who cured him with herbal medicine.

In 2002, he was diagnosed with an incurable GERD or acid reflux disease. Per doctors, he was to avoid a rather long list of favorite food or drinks and to sleep sitting up in bed until his death simply because there was no known cure. He was devastated again. He suffered heavily on an hourly basis for two solid years. There was no permanent solution. He even thought of committing suicide. There was no hope.

Suddenly, he was mysteriously led to a Vietnamese acupuncturist who cured him with herbal food supplements. While picking up the incredible goods off the shelf for him, he recommended him to sleep flat in the bed beginning that night with the first dose in. While thinking of his words to follow or not, he fell asleep flat. Next morning, he realized that no stomach acid came back up at all. He cried so hard.

Based on his experience, he wrote an online column of factual information in Korean to aid those with the same disease once and for all. He had saved quite a few lives out of misery for years, but a sensible stream of crying for help stopped just as he began on this book. The supreme beings must have done it to free him for this project. Enlightening the human beings for our new world would be more urgent.